MISSY

EDITION

X&Y

GENERATION

Z

THE INVISIBLE

ISBN: 978-0-9995147-1-9

Library of Congress Control Number: 2017918635

PRINTED IN THE UNITED STATES OF AMERICA

Book Design & Layout: Russell Lake - SeedStudios.com

First Edition

THE INVISIBLE

7

MISSY PAYNE

GENERATION X&Y EDITION

The odds of Missy completing this book were low. Do you guys know Missy very well? Why don't you just get a camera crew to ride around in the backseat of her car? Her life is a book and TV show combined. Let me give you a couple of examples. It was a regular Wednesday afternoon. She came flying into the gym, hair in a ponytail, shoveling what she considered lunch into her mouth before a parent meeting to address attendance, (or lack thereof) for one of the cheer teams. After that meeting, she sprinted into the bathroom where she began to curl her hair, put on make-up, and change clothes while athletes (contacted only 24 hours prior) began arriving in uniform for a photo shoot with "Survivor Missy" for the local newspaper. I helped throw together a couple of poses while Missy stood center stage amid her fan club of cheerleaders. After the photo shoot, a group of adults arrived at the gym for rehearsal with Missy. You see, she had committed to choreographing a routine for their local elementary school parent's skit. She keeps a lot of balls in the air. Somehow juggling is her forte. But, she was playing her own game of *Survivor* long before she was on the show *Survivor*!

I was given the opportunity to use the *Invisible 7* in a corporate setting with executives, teachers and coaches. By following the curriculum, I was able to make seemingly uncomfortable situations become relatable. As we explored sections on equality and utilized some of the exercises, like the personality compass, you could see light bulbs going off. Participants were able to identify the part they played in helping create equality and how their personalities and the personalities of those they interact with daily can either help or hinder their journey. It became apparent fairly quickly that this book can create "aha" moments from cover to cover.

The interactive part of this book, real world application and challenges found in the *Invisible 7* is what really makes it special. Regardless of age, background, creed, or color, every page of this book is relatable and allows the reader to see the world through new eyes.

Chris Henson

Express Cheer

Owner and CEO

(Missy's business partner - at one point!)

TABLE OF CONTENTS

THANK YOU

The Thank Yous are certainly endless, because no one ever accomplishes success without many hands in the pot. The kids who have been part of our "Cheer 4 Your Life" family, all of our alumni from "The Warriors Project™", and the students and teachers at the Dallas Lutheran School who participated in the test ride, have been an enormous part of this creation. But, to those who have been <u>on</u> *this* train, *this* three-year ride, supporting the completion of *this* book... I give my sincere gratitude:

Mom & Dad - your endless amount of "we are so proud of you" and "that's just wonderful" and "how do you do all you do's" are the perfect parenting tools that someone creative needs to have to not quit.

Bay & Abby – the endless amount of "you should talk to my mom about that," friends that you have brought to me for wisdom, a listening ear, and some parent perspective have been the perfect test subjects for this entire experiment.

Cheryll – the endless amount of words, pages and time you put forth to help write this thing even when I would scrap whole chapters and start over, proved your belief in the impact it's going to have.

Russell – for your endless travel to and from Texas to guide, create, and inspire the vision.

Tracy – the endless amount of love you have shown me through your truth, your guidance, and for always being one step ahead of me.

Chris – for the endless laughs and calling it like it is, and counting 8-counts for me while I wrote.

Katrina – for the endless items you have completed off my to-do list – no matter what they were...

Sam, Gus & Bob – for sharing your endless God-given talents, and giving up part of your Spring Break to create beautiful illustrations.

Taylor – for your endless hours behind the camera, driving me places when I got lost, and for opinions even when I didn't ask for them.

and to GOD – You know why!

INTRODUCTION

So, there I was in the middle of no-where in the country of Nicaragua. Season 29 of the hit reality TV show, *Survivor*, landed me on that remote island with unbelievable daily challenges (and I don't mean "immunity" challenges). How could I possibly make it to each day's sunset without compromising my dignity, integrity, honesty, and loyalty surrounded by strangers filled with envy, spite, and lies? Each castaway arrives with their own pre-conceived ideas and a million-dollar prize at stake. But, as the days pass and the more hungry, tired, and dirty you get, your true colors bleed through. It's impossible to expect players to be on their best behavior – as the viewer forgets – we are all human beings.

For the first time in *Survivor* history, the producers added a Day Zero to our season. So, my game began when my daughter (Baylor) and I were dropped off in the middle of the forest. Seriously? With limited daylight left, we figured we had about two hours to make fire and find shelter.

I began endless attempts to make a fire. We had been given a flint and a striker, but I clearly hadn't grasped the importance of learning how to use them at pre-game camp. Hours passed, darkness set in, and the cameramen assigned to us were so bored they began to disperse! Out of nowhere, came the loudest howling, growling animal sound I have ever heard! Baylor completely flipped out when she heard it—I mean *completely!* These were howler monkeys up in the trees...and an entire family joined us and waited and watched my thousand strikes to get a spark.

Spoiler alert: we didn't (make a fire) and we didn't (find shelter)!

That was the first night of the 39 that I spent in Nicaragua. During my seven-week adventure, away from home and without any contact with family members, my perception of who I was definitely shifted. Because, if you let an experience alter your life, it will.

Long before I played the game of *Survivor*, I was living it out in my daily life. I was the driver in a teen car accident putting one of my best friends in the ICU before I was mature enough to handle that level of responsibility. I had a business yanked out from underneath me, leaving me with only a dozen of the hundreds of young cheerleaders and their families that had been my loyal clients. I had been divorced. I had been a single mom. I had been rich, poor, and broken hearted!

My last divorce hit me like a ton of bricks. Seemingly surviving on the outside, but crumbling on the inside, I pulled up my bootstraps and continued on with my insanely busy last two months of that particular spring. I proceeded to coach my cheer teams through the remainder of that competition season. I finished directing and producing a live musical production, and hosted the party of a lifetime for my Baylor's high school graduation.

It is an interesting phenomenon **when we serve others**, how quickly we can forget our biggest problems and gain such reward witnessing gratitude from those we support. I might've been experiencing an internal crisis but people were counting on me, and I had to deliver.

My *Survivor* – the show - experience was similar. It developed more strength than I knew I had. It opened my eyes to see that the world can make you believe *make believe* things. The human mind is quite amazing, able to be manipulated to change our thoughts and beliefs in a split second. It was a daily feat not to allow this mind-altering experience to have an effect on me. I was certainly being pushed and prodded to play the game as a backstabber, kicking and punching. But, acting like a fool, wasn't worth helping to raise a network's rating point or even a million bucks.

This book is my "million dollar" prize!

My take away from *Survivor* became the foundation of the book, the backbone for the Warriors Project™, and the reason behind Cheer 4 Your Life 501(c)3, which I established to give financial support to teenagers needing help.

My #1 hope is that this book will help you gain a new perspective:

about yourself;

about your family and friends;

about co-worker's lives.

And, that you will choose a journey that could positively affect change...

EVERYWHERE!

With our current trend of lightning speed technology, there are also some forgotten human instincts – like how to speak to one another. Texting and social media, Siri and Alexa have given us all excuses to quit having *real* conversations. And, the self-thinking, self-motivated, self-disciplined *world-changing* abilities of the millennials is literally off the charts. I have become accustomed to using social media and texting as a means of communication for the simplicity factor. But, I still believe that it is my duty as a Gen X-er to model behaviors and lifestyles that our parents and grandparents passed down to us. And it can be accomplished through one simple philosophy:

Service...to others.

It's as simple as that.

The sky is the limit.

And that is because there will always be a need, there will always be an opportunity. It is a virtual well of possibility that will never run dry.

It is almost unbelievable *all the good* that can come from volunteering at a homeless shelter, or restocking the books at your local library, or helping out with a special needs programs, or any one of hundreds of community outreach programs. If we do it, they will too!

Giving to others truly is the cure-all pill for what ails us individually and as a society—so much so that you can't help but wonder why it isn't an integral part of our public education systems and corporations. Service to others is the embodiment of what Albert Schweitzer said long before smart phones and Facebook became part of our cultural landscape:

"The only really happy people are those who have learned how to serve."

Until service programs are a mainstream part of most of our lives, I am doing my part to help promote the culture of giving back. It may not change the entire world but it will change *someone's* world.

As a first step, I have identified seven key character-building qualities that lie dormant in each of us.

These qualities are:

Equality	**Self-Discipline**
Humility	**Compassion**
Integrity	**Generosity**
Resilience	

Your character is the sum of all the qualities that make you who you are: your values, your thoughts, your words, your actions. You already carry each of "the Invisible 7" inside your heart and soul. And, whether you are totally aware of your day to day utilization of them or not, I would like to offer an adventurous way for you to activate each one. As you move from focusing on one trait to the next, you will learn more about yourself, about working with others, and learn to develop a savvy approach to dealing with relationships, tasks, and opportunities.

When we're prepared to give to others, it helps us have a better understanding of ourselves—our beliefs, morals, motivations, and what ultimately shapes our perspective. My hope for you is that, when you have completed the challenges in the book and thoughtfully answered the questions, you will be a changed person—a person who recognizes their own potential *and* the amazing potential you have to help and serve others. To effect change—however you go about it—requires vision and commitment and a hope for a better future. I'm here to help you every step of the way.

Special Instructions

Throughout the book I have included QR codes that link to special videos. You can access the video by using the camera on your smartphone or tablet device along with a QR code reader. Most are free and can be found in the App Store or Google Play.

On your mark...Get set...GO!

GENERATION X&Y EDITION

EQUALITY

My *Survivor* Story...

To say the cast of my season on *Survivor* was diverse would be a HUGE understatement. I was thrown into a group of people on that island of Nicaragua who were as diverse a group as you could *ever imagine*. Since it was a couples' season filled with partners who were married, dating, or blood relatives, there is no doubt this concept added some serious complexity to the game. It naturally created a two-against-two platform as well as an increased level of emotion—just what the producers wanted.

On Day Nineteen we were given a Reward Challenge (the type that usually offers the winners comfort in the form of food, drink, or items you want for camp). At this point, we were no longer on tribes, and it was every man or woman for themselves. Teams were divided by drawing rocks for captains who then chose players. For that Reward Challenge,

I was the odd man out and not chosen to play. This was partly due to my age and strength in comparison to the younger women still in the game. Even though I could understand this logically, it brought up feelings of anger, frustration and helplessness! After all, I had the same *inner* strength they had, and I certainly had more wisdom and ability to strategize for a victory! But none of that mattered; **I was left out!** And, first thing that came to my mind was, *"This is so unfair!"*

I sat and watched as my daughter's team got beaten (which was the team I assumed I would have been competing on had I been chosen). So, what was the lesson here? Patience? Understanding? Fight for yourself? I considered telling the losing team members, "I told ya so?! Now, you guys don't get to eat at the Survivor Taco Bar and neither do I!" I was definitely *thinking* these things but in the end decided my comments probably wouldn't have been too well received right after the defeat. So, I bit my tongue.

Being left out of this one competition really drove home this point: Quite often at the heart of our frustration from being treated unequally lies fear—

> *fear of missing out*
> *fear of others getting ahead*
> *fear of others not recognizing your worth.*

After all, who wants to be left out? Or to be told 'you're not good enough' or that someone else can do it better than you?

The more experiences I have in life, the more I come to realize that most of the time whenever I feel belittled, the other people involved aren't focused on me *at all*. They are worried about their own stakes in the game and their own successes. This is true if you're on a tiny island with strangers on a reality TV show or working on a presentation for a client or chairing your child's school fundraiser. *People focus mostly on themselves.*

I know in many ways we're all unique and individual. I also know that at our core, we all experience the same feelings (i.e. anger, sadness, shame, guilt, love, passion, and joy). No matter how or where you were raised, your family or marital status, or how well you're doing in your career, you really are on an equal playing field with everyone else when it comes to shared emotions. Just like my experience on Survivor with men and women from all kinds of different backgrounds—socioeconomically, racially, morally, and ethnically—I realized that in spite of these dramatic differences, we all share something in common: **the desire to be valued!**

Definition of Equality
Dealing fairly and equally with all concerned

What Does It Mean to Be Treated Equally?

Have you ever done the majority of the work on a major pitch for a new client, but others took the credit? Or, have you ever been left out of the *decision makers club* for a committee or charity because you didn't buy into the social politics?

Sometimes these slights can be unintended and with no ill feelings directed towards you; other times they're truly intentional and you're the one who catches all the fall-out. Either way, it doesn't feel very fair!

And you know what? You're right.

It may not be fair or equitable that your career path has had a few unfortunate setbacks or that you're still paying back an overwhelming student loan while everyone else seems to be getting ahead financially...*way ahead.* But then again, does it seem fair or equal that you just seem to have a natural ability to connect with clients and co-workers? It's also not fair that the coach's kid gets to play the full game even though your daughter is a better, faster player!

Regardless of what you think about yourself or your current circumstances, we all have commonalities of feelings. We show them (or hide them) differently, but underneath the face we present to the world, we all share many of the same feelings.

That's what makes us human. We are all feeling, hurting, this-isn't-fair make-it-right humans that *all* share in the basic emotions of life. Sure, a coworker may seem to be hitting his sales numbers out of the park, but underneath the high-end business suit, he's still a guy who wants what you want—**to be valued** for who he is; not just how much money he's making for the company.

The same is true of the overly involved mom in the Parent-Teacher Organization. She may be spending so many evenings at school painting scenery for the 4th grade play because her home life is less than stellar. She's looking for validation and respect wherever she can find it.

It's the human condition: at the very core of each of us, we are all basically the same. Take away the details of our lives—where we live, what we drive, what our family is like—and all we are left with is what's inside a person and their need to be valued, loved, respected, and treated equally. That's it.

ACTIVITY: The better understanding you have of who you are, the easier life becomes when relating to others. When you need to collaborate on a work project or when you join a committee, you should look for "like-minded" people to be on your team. You can identify their personality types after you gain some clarity about yours...

The Personality Compass quick test helps you identify your strengths. Though you may display some of the characteristics in all four areas, there will be a distinct difference in your most dominant and your weakest type. Should you attempt to balance the two? That depends on what impact you currently have in your relationships (i.e. friends, family, project groups, athletic teams, extracurricular activities).

A variation of The Personality Compass
Mini Quiz

Complete the following sentences honestly by circling either a, b, c or d. Even though you might sometimes have multiple characteristics, choose only one for the purposes of this exercise.

1. As a young child of four or five, I *most* often _____ in order to get what I wanted.

    a. got at least a little bit upset

    b. made a plan that just might work

    c. became a voluntary little helper

    d. acted really cute and charming

2. By age ten, I was *most* likely thought of as a _____ by my peers.

    a. competitor (who put in the extra effort to be, or to have, the best)

    b. thinker (who added the details in order for projects to work properly)

    c. peacemaker (who encouraged everyone to get along together)

    d. thrill-seeker (who was an inspiration to all for trying new things)

3. Regarding my long-term future, I am *most* interested in _____.

   a. reaching my career goals with an admirable level of success

   b. learning and building a reputation for doing excellent work

   c. making sure my values stay high and my conscience clear

   d. living my dreams of free-spirited, exciting adventure

4. My body language is *most* easily recognizable by my _____.

   a. take-charge presence

   b. perfect posture

   c. sincere smile

   d. relaxed attitude

5. The *most* accurate motto for my having a stress-free life could be: _____.

   a. 'do it to win'

   b. 'do it right the first time'

   c. 'do it as a team'

   d. 'do it for fun'

6. People who know me well would probably view my *main* strength as my _____.

   a. confidence

   b. logic

   c. compassion

   d. energy

7. When having to make a decision, I *usually* prefer to
do it _____ .

   a. quickly

   b. analytically

   c. cooperatively

   d. creatively

8. *More* often than not, I like to work in a _____
environment.

   a. challenging

   b. structured

   c. friendly

   d. changing

9. The *easiest* leadership style for me is _____ .

   a. telling others what needs to be done, with a
deadline time for finishing

   b. persuading people with facts, as to why things
should be done a certain way

   c. sharing my own leadership roles, and all
workloads, among those involved

   d. experimenting with new and different ways of
doing almost anything

10. As a leader, I probably value and am the most naturally gifted at _____.

   a. establishing the purpose and mission of a group

   b. clarifying the rules and requirements that all in a group must follow

   c. finding out people's individual needs and concerns within a group

   d. motivating participants to *want* to carry out the group commitments

11. As far back as I can remember, I have *mostly* received respect for my _____.

   a. task or sports accomplishments

   b. organizational or scholastic honors

   c. community contributions or selfless acts

   d. artistic or entertainment endeavors

Tally your score here:

A = _____

B = _____

C = _____

D = _____

The 'answer codes' for the 11 questions are as follows:

    a. All a answers indicate a NORTH tendency.

    b. All b answers indicate an EAST tendency.

    c. All c answers indicate a SOUTH tendency.

    d. All d answers indicate a WEST tendency.

Not all NORTHS, for example, will have only NORTH answers; but they will have more NORTH answers than any of the others...and so on with E, S, W. Whatever direction receives the most answers indicates the likelihood that you are dominant in that nature.

See the chart on the next page.

NORTH: Gets the Job done FAST!
Natural Leader • Goal-Centered • Fast-paced • Task- oriented • Assertive •
Decisive • Confident • Determined • Competitive • Independent

**WEST: Expands
All Horizons**

Natural Risk-Taker
Idea-Centered
Creative
Innovative
Flexible
Visionary
Spontaneous
Enthusiastic
Free-Spirited
Energetic

**EAST: Does it
Right the First
Time**

Natural Planner
Quality-centered
Analytical
Organized
Logical
Focused
Exact
Perfectionist
Productive
Structured

SOUTH: Builds the Best Teams
Natural Team Player • Process-Centered • Slow-paced •
Good listener • Non-confrontational • Sensitive • Patient •
Understanding • Generous • Helpful

TRY THIS If you're in a group setting, divide into teams using the results from the Personality Compass Quiz. If not, it's okay, you can still play. Check out this video for what's next:

Equality Challenge #1

For one day, leave your car at home and take public transportation. Try it on a work day, or on a Saturday to the grocery store and back. If you are familiar with your local transit route, congratulations. But, I was not! The first time I did this challenge it took me over 2 hours just to get close to the store. It established an unpredictable appreciation for those who don't have a car. Post any videos/ pics and your comments on Instagram (#invisible7) and/or upload to [http://theinvisible7.com] and upon completion receive **20 points!**

"I say to you today, my friends, so even though we face the difficulties of today and tomorrow, I still have a dream. It is a dream deeply rooted in the American dream.
I have a dream that one day this nation will rise up and live out the true meaning of its creed: 'We hold these truths to be self-evident: that all men are created equal.'" — Martin Luther King, Jr.

When you're making attempts to create fairness, it is important to consider individuality and the unique qualities in each person. Speak up for the benefit of your company, your PTA, or your community organization to assist in plugging folks into their best fit. When people are given tasks within their talent zone and are viewed as an integral part of the collective effort, satisfaction and personal investment increases and equality (or lack thereof) ceases to be a significant problem.

Albert Einstein once claimed "Everybody is a genius. But if you judge a fish by its ability to climb a tree, it will live its whole life believing that it is stupid." Sometimes others have to achieve things in a different manner than you do!

Equality Challenge #2

Interview an adult with a physical handicap (i.e. confined to a wheelchair, without a limb, blind...) due to disease or permanent injury. Are they treated differently than their able-bodied friends? What do they wish everyone knew about them? (Note: Challenge #1 and #2 could be completed at the same time.)

Take a picture of the person you interview and add a few comments about the most surprising or inspiring thing you learned from them. Post any videos/ pics and your comments on Instagram (#invisible7) and/or upload to [http://theinvisible7.com] and upon completion receive **10 points!**

Remember This...

When we treat others as our equals, regardless of their circumstances, race, gender, title, or education, we level the relationship playing field and increase the opportunity for stronger friendships and a deeper investment in our company or organization's culture.

When people believe they are being valued for their contribution, their perception of everything changes. There is no single benefit when equality is present in a company, a team, or a crew of volunteers; there are Many.

This is What Happened to Me!

When I was a sophomore in high school, I was the only one of my friends who had a driver's license. It was a provisional one that I was able to get because my godfather was the county judge of Dallas who had a say so. Because it was provisional, my license came with some limitations. Under the terms, I could only drive to and from school and to and from work (even though I didn't have a job). On top of the legal restrictions, my father made it extremely clear that I was not allowed to drive someone else's car because our insurance didn't cover that.

It was a beautiful Sunday afternoon and my friend Kim's dad said, "Hey, why don't y'all take my convertible for a spin since Missy has her license and can drive?" When he tossed me the keys, every single rule from dad and all the guidelines from the State of Texas for my provisional license quickly faded. I climbed in with my three friends and we drove away. Our first stop was the carwash to visit our boyfriends and to show off that car. When we headed back towards the house, the radio was blaring, and all of us were engaged in age appropriate dancing and singing. Kim was seated on top of the headrest of the passenger seat and Beth and Leslie were almost sitting on top of the trunk (since there really was no back seat).

It wasn't when I turned left that they all fell out. It was *after the left turn* when I accelerated that I heard "Miiiissssssyyyyyyyy." When I turned around all I remember seeing were six legs as their bodies went airborne. I was so shocked at what I saw that I kept driving about 40 yards afterwards. I just couldn't process what had just happened.

The only thing I remember is the sound of sirens and police cars speeding up to the scene.

After the emergency team got Leslie stabilized and into the ambulance, I heard them ask, "Who was driving?" I raised my hand and two cops escorted me to their car, handcuffed me, and put me in the backseat. As if it wasn't already traumatizing enough to see one of your best friends covered in blood and the other two banged up, an audience of my high school peers began arriving just in time to see me being driven away in a police car.

My parents came to get me at the station. I remember my dad's protective and concerned inquiries, like 'it seems that they *all* could be categorized as irresponsible'?! It was at that moment that I realized I was possibly being treated a bit *unfairly*. I was getting all the blame because I was the driver. I was accused of being drunk, being mad at my girlfriends and intentionally causing them to fall out, and deliberately driving recklessly, but none of the accusations were accurate. The simple truth was that as a fifteen-year-old, I didn't have enough experience to understand the potential consequence of getting behind the wheel of that extremely powerful and fast car.

For the next three weeks, I visited my friend Leslie every day in the hospital where she would ask me, "What happened?" and "Who was driving?" over and over and over again. She had hit her head so hard that she suffered short-term memory loss and couldn't remember the details of the accident. At school each day, people would ask, "So, is it true you were drinking and driving?" or "Were you really angry at your friends?" The list of stupid questions people asked me went on for months after the accident. Not surprisingly, my new provisional license was suspended and I wasn't allowed to drive again until I turned sixteen, some seven months later.

I was so thankful my friends weren't seriously hurt but I also remember thinking at the time, "Man, life can be so unfair!" It was a life lesson in assuming responsibility while wishing for a do-over that I'll never forget.

Equality Challenge #3

Establish a day of equality at work or with any other group in which you're involved (i.e. your tennis team, Bible study, Dad's club). Schedule a day when you will all be together for everyone to wear the *same* shirt, or at least assign the same color. Upon arrival that day, give everyone a name tag to wear with an "E" written on it. Bring a homemade treat and distribute to each person. Don't explain, just observe. Does this create a more energetic environment? Are there any people that surprised you for actually participating?

Post any videos/ pics and your comments on Instagram (#invisible7) and/or upload to [http://theinvisible7.com] and upon completion receive **15 points!**

How Will This Benefit Me?

Consider this: there are people who work alongside you that may appear to have it all together, but outside the office, their lives are a struggle. Maybe their marriage is falling apart or their kid is having problems. Or maybe the go-to, get-it-done person in your organization seems to be 'everything to everyone,' but is neglecting her dysfunctional relationship at home.

You truly never know what's going on in someone else's life—regardless of how things appear outwardly. Focusing on equality is a biggie in terms of building your character traits. Look around at work, at home, at one of your committee meetings. I imagine if the bossiest, the quietest, and the most obnoxious person could find common ground, the vibe would change immensely. Remember, everyone carries with them the same feelings and desires to be valued—no matter their pay grade or how many volunteer hours they've logged.

It's easy to get overwhelmed with the challenge of trying to overcome inequality. But it's a process that begins simple enough: Just treat the next person you meet as an equal.

And then the next.

And the next.

Not Convinced?

"Equality is a trait viewed differently by different people, which makes it a bit difficult. When I was on *Survivor* treating people equally without bias came only after you proved that you could compete. Being an older player, I was able to change their perception with my determination and inner strength–and was treated equally.

Similarly, at the Warriors Games,™ you are an equal part of a team, but you are one member that works with others to achieve the final goal. Everyone comes to the games with their own values, and that's what makes it so special. One teenager named Colby pushed himself out of his comfort zone especially when it came down the fire making challenge.

This program is all about learning what everyone brings with them and helping them to succeed even more!"

———

Carolyn Rivera
Survivor – Season 30
Orlando, FL

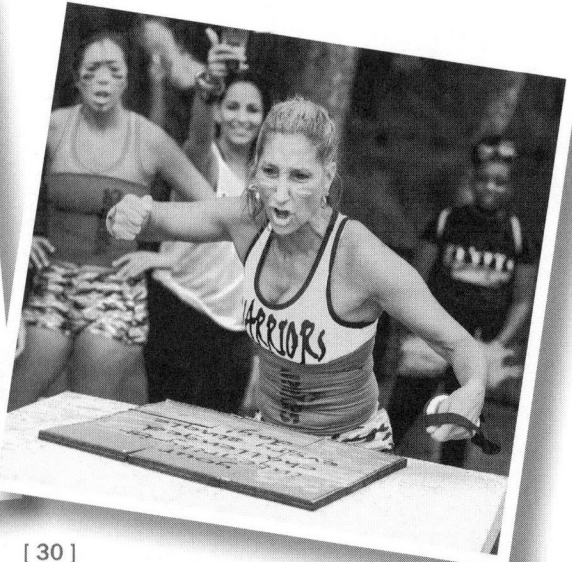

T.P.Q.'s

o   Have you ever been treated differently for being late
    to a meeting than someone else who was also late?

o   Do you find it easy or difficult to become a team
    player in a group at work or on a volunteer
    committee?

o   Can you identify (in any aspect) similarities with
    a co-worker, or group member who appears to be
    dramatically different than you? What would you
    need to know about that person to be able to level the
    playing field?

Use this space to make notes and personal thoughts about EQUALITY.

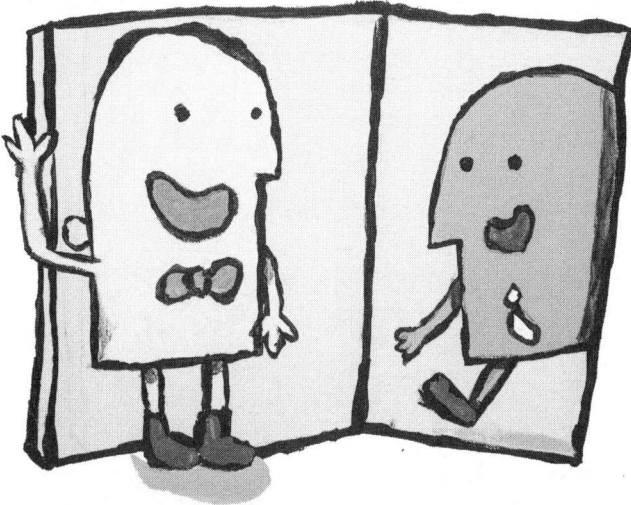

HUMILITY

HUMILITY

My *Survivor* Story...

Water challenges were my favorite ones on *Survivor* for a couple of reasons. First, I've always been a great swimmer and second, it was so refreshing to get out of the heat and into the cool saltwater. One of our Reward Challenges required us to retrieve keys and climb over a floating tower and then swim them to a dock where there was a locked box with puzzle pieces inside. It was a great challenge but sadly, my team lost.

The reward to the winning team was a trip to visit a local village and distribute brand new baseball uniforms and equipment to kids in the league who desperately needed them. Producers behind the scenes at *Survivor* are great about forming partnerships with the community where they are filming during each season.

I wanted to take part in this reward as much as I wanted a shower! You can imagine my sadness when our team lost the challenge. I was devastated.

But not for long.

In a surprising moment, my nemesis on the winning team, Reed, announced to Jeff that he wanted to trade places with me and give me his spot for this particular reward. I was shocked. (I didn't care at the time, but I eventually realized he was working an agenda to win over the players he would be with back at camp.) Still, I was humbly taken aback! I bear-hugged him and cried on his shoulder. I was so grateful! We switched spots and I swam off the dock with the other victors.

When we arrived on the scene, the producers handed us giant duffel bags filled with bats, balls, mitts, jerseys and shorts. We walked onto the field and were greeted by about fifty teens filled with excitement as if it were Christmas. It was as if Santa Claus had parked his sleigh right on the pitcher's mound!

This was my very favorite experience of all thirty-nine days.

After we gave the kids their new equipment, they suited up to play a game. We were given a bunch of junk food (I was the only one who cared that it wasn't healthy) and we got to sit in the stands with their parents, siblings, and other locals from the village and cheer for them.

This was my only opportunity to see real life in the impoverished country of Nicaragua, because I made it so far in the game. It was a humbling experience to glance around at the surroundings and notice the half-built houses with tarps for roofs, laundry hanging on makeshift clotheslines, and chickens and goats (which I'm pretty sure weren't pets!) in fenced-in front yards. It was a reminder of how blessed my life has been and how much I have taken for granted. I will cherish that memory and the smiles on those kid's faces when they received our gifts, forever!

Definition of Humility

A modest view of one's own importance; humbleness

What Does it Mean to Exhibit Humility?

Humility is often one of the most misunderstood characteristics of humans. Many people have a misperception about what it means to be humble or to act with humility.

Is it a good thing or a bad thing?

Is it considered a sign of strength or weakness?

Is it admired or mocked? (After all, isn't it related to humiliate? And what could possibly be good about that?) True humility is one of the greatest strengths anyone can possess. It's one of those crazy personality traits hard to define but easy to see.

Throughout history, humility has often been the hallmark of some of our most effective and dynamic leaders. To be humble, truly humble, means doing what is right and putting the welfare of others above yourself. It means doing the behind-the-scene grunt work. Sometimes it even means not revealing everything you know about someone or some situation in order to protect them—even at the expense of your own status. It frequently means not always getting credit for all your efforts and sometimes sharing the spotlight with those who have contributed far less than you have.

Think of the highest producer at the office. Or, what about the parent who leads the charge in the annual fundraiser? Do they talk about what they did to create individual success? Or, do they include the supporting committee in their comments? If so, that's a humble approach. Whatever successes or victories we experience, we have the opportunity to shine the spotlight solely on our own efforts and accomplishments or humbly redirect it towards the scads of people who've helped us along the way.

Every day—in lots of ways—we have the choice to model humility.

Or not.

From success on sports teams, in the working world, and in relationships, it is the wise, wise person who understands and recognizes that no one—not a single soul—gets by completely on his own. No matter the brains, the athletic ability, or social status, all of us have support systems that touch our lives in lots of ways. Some people affect us in big, spectacular ways; others in just occasional or considerably less significant ways.

It's time to experience first-hand what this feels like. Today, you are going to be challenged to reach out to someone who isn't directly in your circle of friends. Maybe you see them at work every day, but this isn't someone you would normally hang out with in the break room. Or, this person is not someone you would probably take to dinner outside regular work functions.

Once you have an idea of who you will choose, check out this video for what's next:

Humility Challenge #1

Create an outline showing the breakdown of the people who support your successful endeavors. There's a supportive network of folks who you interact with daily. Have you ever noticed how many people (paid or not) are part of that chain?

For example, who does your laundry? Who does the repairs on your car? Who supplies you with copies, or a Power Point for that weekly staff meeting?

Post a picture of your list and your comments on Instagram (#invisible7) and/or upload to [http://theinvisible7.com] and upon completion receive **10 points**!

Our country, our society as a whole, is doomed without the presence of humility. A humble heart has the ability to change someone's words and thoughts and actions for the betterment of everyone. One person with healthy humility may only affect one person each day, but performed consistently, that adds up to thousands of people over a lifetime.

For many famous athletes and celebrities, the more well-known they are, the more accomplished they become, and the more they command in salaries, the less inclined they are to exhibit humility. The superstars who can control their tendency to become arrogant after they exceed a million likes on one of their posts are the ones who earn genuine respect from fans.

Fortunately, there are some stellar examples that give us some hope that both extraordinary success and humility can coexist:

- Peyton Manning is arguably the best quarterback in the NFL yet he still turned down an extra $1.4 million per year when he signed with the Denver Broncos saying simply, "I don't deserve it." In addition to turning down the extra cash, Manning has donated more than $6.5 million to at-risk children throughout his career and was so supportive of the children's hospital at St. Vincent's in Indianapolis that they named it after him.

- Johnny Depp usually travels with his Captain Jack Sparrow costume from the "Pirates of the Caribbean" movies so that he can visit children's hospitals wherever he is visiting or working.

Humility Challenge #2

[This is a great opportunity for a group outing.]

Make arrangements to volunteer with your city's sanitation department, a homeless shelter, the welfare office, the library, county-run hospital, or animal services. What role does humility play in effectively serving in this position?

Post any videos/ pics and your comments on Instagram (#invisible7) and/or upload to [http://theinvisible7.com] and upon completion receive **20 points**!

Remember This...

o Confucius defined humility as "the solid foundation of all virtues."

o Being humble gives you the courage to try new things.

o "True humility is not thinking less of yourself; it is thinking of yourself less." – C. S. Lewis

This is What Happened to Me

I was 26 years old, I was getting a divorce and moving back home to Dallas with a 10-month-old baby. I had landed a teaching job briefly while in Colorado which caught the interest of my old middle school teacher back in Texas. She called and said that the school district where I had graduated from was looking for a new drama teacher. I was so excited! It was exactly what my college degree had earned me. And, I was thrilled to be back on my home turf.

I was hired late Spring for the following school year. It wasn't until early Summer that I was informed I wouldn't be teaching Drama class after all...instead it would be Speech. Speech?!? The department head, who was also the drama teacher decided she would take all the current drama classes. She handed me a very dusty notebook from a top shelf in her office with the Speech curriculum that had "formerly been utilized" for their middle school speech classes. I wanted to quit! I couldn't imagine in that moment how I could possibly make this *boring* class into something great. So, I asked permission from my principal (who was my former English teacher) if I could take a stab at re-writing the curriculum. "Of course," she said, "Just make certain it follows the guidelines of the Texas Education Knowledge and Skills." (which is the standard guidelines for Texas public schools).

I dove in. I spent countless hours re-inventing Speech class. I researched other schools' offerings, and found that Speech programs had teams. Competitive teams! Now we were talking. By the first day of school, I had written Speech

1, 2 and 3 (just in case it was to grow). I had convinced the school to buy a little more up to date textbook. And I had tryouts for the Speech team.

By the middle of that semester, there was a waiting list for Spring, I had a full team of competitors, and I had created the school newscast which aired in the cafeteria daily! Oh, and I did end up using that Speech 3 curriculum eventually.

I realized that the students were excited to have a new energy at the school. I struck the match, but they took the spark and turned it into a forest fire. It was my favorite class I ever taught.

The lesson I learned: being humbled can help create strength. It wasn't how I wanted to gain strength at that moment, but I had two choices after that humbling experience: grow from it and be stronger or be defeated by it and let it affect my self-worth.

I chose to grow!

I also learned that transparent communication can help change the course of your life. By simply asking for what I wanted, I ended up with a beautiful end product that positively affected my students' lives forever (their words, not mine).

Humility Challenge #3

Choose up to seven people, including some at work and some at home, to whom you owe an apology. Write a note and say, "I apologize for..." describing in a few short words, why. Make it a hand-written note that you can hide in their desk, in their car, or have it personally delivered by someone else. Sign the notes, keep yourself out of the spotlight if possible, and let them react in their own way and on their own timeline.

Post any videos/ pics (possibly of their reaction) and your comments on Instagram (#invisible7) and/or upload to [http://theinvisible7.com] and upon completion receive **15 points**!

How Will This Benefit Me?

When you think of Benjamin Franklin, you probably remember the balding guy with the shaggy side hair and the tiny, wire-framed glasses known for the whole electricity experiment with the kite and key. In his early twenties, however, Franklin was known somewhat as an abrasive, never-admit-defeat debater. No matter the subject or the facts, Franklin went out of his way to berate and belittle those he disagreed with just to prove his debating skills.

In short, he was a total jerk.

But once he got past his know-it-all twenties and after an older gentleman pointed out Ben's prideful and arrogant nature, ol' Ben set out on a lifelong quest to strengthen every aspect of his character.

The result: he began practicing humility.

Franklin sought to mend his ways. Instead of using words as weapons, he resolved to make conversational peace whenever possible.

As a young man, Franklin quickly realized the many benefits of working towards engaging others without so much concern for making his voice heard. What he found, almost immediately, was that when he listened to others, they listened to him. This practice went on for the rest of Franklin's life, including his presence at the 1787 Constitutional Convention. At eighty-one years old, Franklin was credited with saying about the document, "The opinions I have had of its errors, I sacrifice to the public good." In other words, he knew there were a few points over which he disagreed, but considered it in everyone's best interest to forgo his objections. After that, he urged those present to offer their unanimous favor and sign the Constitution.

Not Convinced?

"Humility opens the gateway to personal growth. During my journey competing on *The Amazing Race*, I was often faced with situations that tested my human nature. I learned quickly that self importance and arrogance would lead me to certain failure.

I believe that the space where genuine humility exists is where heroes are born. The Warriors program creates that heroic space. The challenges are humbling and create selflessness in each participant. Donating their time to the community and fundraising for teens in need brings hope and inspires others to do the same.

Joyful PARTICIPATION is the foundation of true learning.

Humble SERVICE proves to inspire hope.

Selfless GIVING always lifts the spirits of the recipient and the witness."

———

Uchenna Agu
The Amazing Race - Season 7 Winner
Houston, Texas

T.P.Q.'s

○ Are the types of people you're naturally drawn to the ones who are open-minded and receptive to you and your ideas, or are they quick to tell you how and where you're wrong or misinformed?

○ Do you look for ways to help others accomplish their tasks even if it means extra hours and work for you? Why or why not?

○ Are you able to be transparent with people you work or volunteer with? If not, is there one new person you could re-invent yourself with?

T.P.Q.'s

o Have you had others take credit for work you've
   done or been blamed for things you didn't do?
   How did you handle it?

o Who is considered to have a 'lesser' position/title
   in your organization that you could help out? What
   could you do for them without them anonymously?

In LIFE...
there will be SUCCESS and Failure,
CELEBRATION and Disappointment.
How will YOU choose to deal with it?

Activity: ICKY STICKYS

Goal: discovering who you are

Materials needed:

A large sheet of blank paper (I like to use newspaper print paper.)

One pad of sticky notes.

Pen or pencil.

A trash can.

Instructions:

Grab a partner and ask them to draw an outline of you on the paper. (I like to tape these to the wall for a hard surface, and stand for the person to outline me.) If you don't have a partner... sketch an outline of a body – from the head to the waist.

(nothing fancy...)!

Use the sticky notes and write descriptive words that you believe about yourself (one word per note) as well as words that others use to describe you.

On the inside of the sketch, place sticky note words that are your perspective of you. On the outside of the sketch, place sticky note words that other people would use to describe you.

Are there any similarities?

Do you have more "positive" words inside or outside? Why?

Which words are things that you can control about yourself?

Which describe your circumstances?

Remove ANY word that is a negative and take it off the paper. Are those words necessary to keep (since you probably can't change that *thing* about you), or can they be removed for good?

It is your family belief system that forms who you are (your personality), but it is your decision to make choices to create who you become (your character). Your life experiences will determine some of your values.

Is it time to make a shift?

Decide which sticky notes should be tossed and throw them in the trash can!

Once you are fairly certain you have made the best word choices, remove the sticky notes one by one and write the word in it's place on the paper. If you have some iffies, leave that word as a sticky and review it the next time,

and the next time,

and the next time,

until you are confident that's the word you want to use.

I like to write my directional word from the Personality Compass quick test at the top and utilize some of those words to get my wheels rolling.

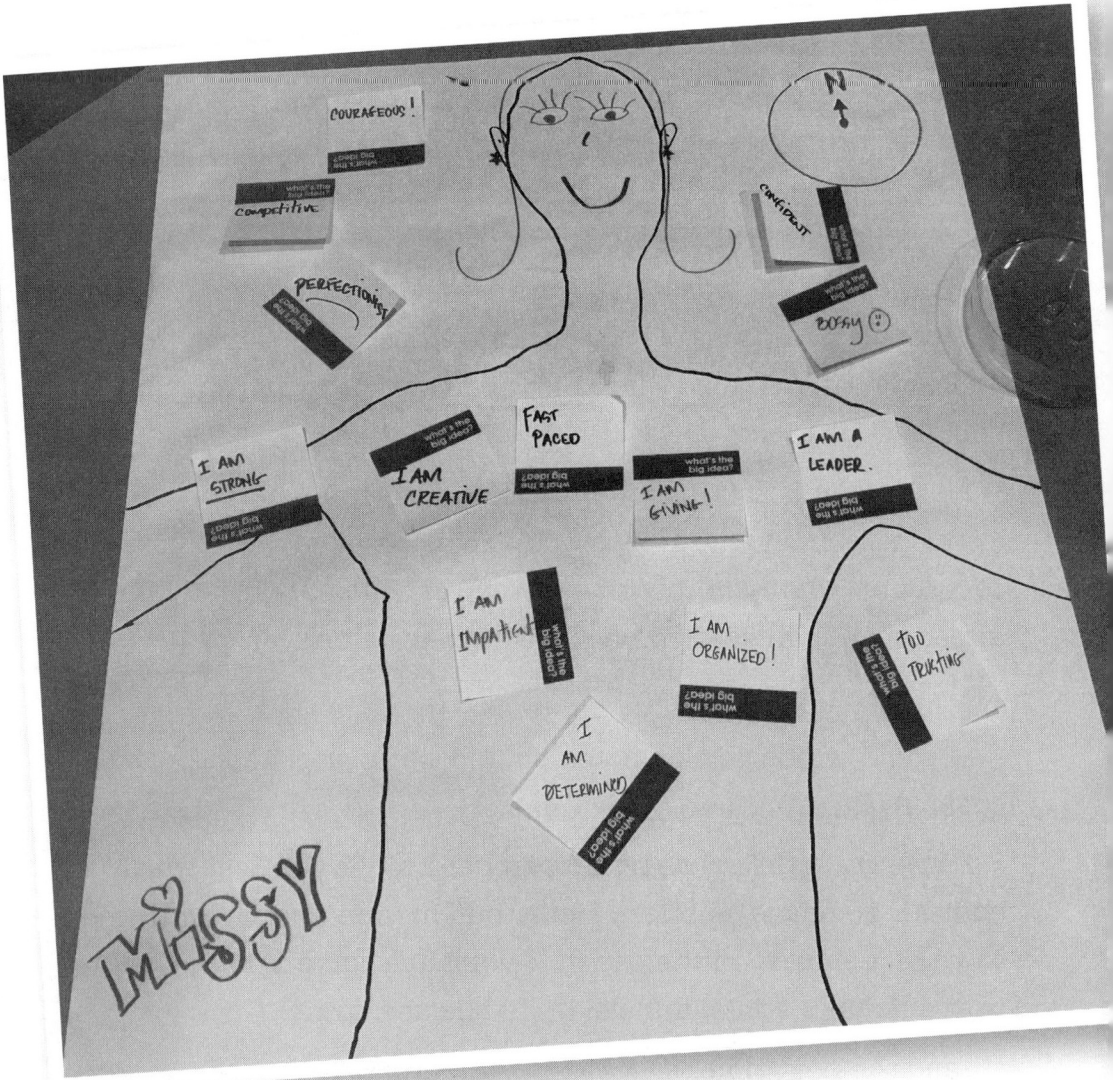

Use this space to make notes and personal thoughts about HUMILITY.

GENERATION **X&Y** EDITION

INTEGRITY

My *Survivor* Story...

My brother was a Lieutenant Commander in the United States Navy. He served our country for many years in a respected position that gave him endless opportunities to display his courage, honor, and integrity for the men and women he worked with daily. I'm grateful for his service to our country and the example he sets for me in so many ways. I think the world of him.

After my family and friends gathered to watch the final episode of my season on *Survivor*, he said, "You made it to the Final Three without jeopardizing your integrity." Wow! That was the greatest compliment I could have received that night.

You see, on *Survivor* there is backstabbing, deceit, lies, and doing whatever it takes to help you survive day in and day out. Even though everyone tries their best not to be affected by the outwit, outplay, outlast atmosphere, it starts out tough and gets nothing but tougher with each passing day. Despite your best efforts, your feelings get in the way. You want to retaliate against those out to get you. You want to respond in a way that brings the most damage to those who challenge you. You want to kick and hit and undermine those who seem to want to hurt you the most.

Still, I had great poll position—I was the oldest female of my season and that gave me the tremendous advantage of perspective. I had years of life experiences in my back pocket that would ultimately serve me very well. I also had the wisdom of people who had poured into me all my life—chief amongst them, my grandmother.

One of the principles I learned from Granny was the importance of not burning bridges when moving on from a relationship, a job, a school—wherever. "You never know when you might see that person again and need something from them," she used to tell me. With her voice ringing in my ears and the constant reminder that former and current students and athletes that I coached would be watching my every word on national television, no less! —my motivation throughout the whole experience was to NOT jeopardize my integrity.

I did my best to be kind to everyone, even the guys who threw fiery torches at me and were constantly plotting against me at every turn. This worked well for me on so many levels because I was being true to myself, was speaking and acting honorably (most of the time!), and I kept moving on to the next challenge.

Until...

I had had the upper hand at every tribal council except the one when my daughter was voted off. The night Baylor's torch was snuffed, it really drove home the feeling of being the one not wanted—it was personal. It was a terrible feeling and I hurt for my girl.

I quickly came to realize that confidence was not the best approach to tribal council; humility was. A dose of indifference was helpful too. When someone would ask me, "Am I going home tonight?" I honestly could respond, "I don't know," because no one knew until the moment of voting. I did my best not to cause others to doubt me or themselves. I told people what I knew to be true and left it at that. Throughout the many seasons of 'Survivor,' I've watched contestants get caught up in the mind games and the double- and triple-crossing of one another to the point where they aren't protecting their own integrity and being true to themselves.

It happens on Survivor and it happens in real life, too.

Throughout my thirty-nine days on Survivor, the temptation to seek revenge and plot all sorts of deceitful and spiteful activities literally surrounded me every second. And again, Granny's words gave me direction. Throughout my childhood and still to this day, she always said, "Treat others as you would like to be treated." Simple words that make living a life of integrity light years easier. If you don't want it done to you or said about you, don't do it or say it about someone else. That's it!

The days and nights on *Survivor* were brutal to say the least. The payoff for the winner—a million dollars! —was crazy, change-your-life money.

But in the end, I came to realize there was no lie or no compromise of my integrity that was worth any amount of money. When I intentionally worked to let kindness and honor guide my words and actions, I could keep my personal integrity intact, even under some pretty extreme conditions. And the coolest aspect about the whole integrity gig is that it works whether you're on a deserted island, in the corporate world, or volunteering alongside others.

Definition of Integrity

Quality of being honest and fair; having strong moral principles and being of good character

What Does it Mean to Live with Integrity?

First and foremost, let's get real: your integrity is challenged every single day! Let's say, you leave the office for lunch. Your co-worker mentions that there's an incredible sale at your favorite store, or your buddy calls and asks you to meet him for 9 holes. Temptation! It's part of our makeup. So, do you call the office and say you've got a flat tire? Or, do you just detour on the way back, hoping nobody will really notice? Either way, even the consideration will jeopardize your integrity. It sounds like a pretty silly example, but whether that has been your experience or there was another instance... you wouldn't have done what you said you were going to do.

Look at a more obvious situation: cheating. These days... cheating on a spouse or girlfriend/boyfriend is larger than life. Cheating to climb the corporate ladder, or borrowing an idea from someone to take credit has the same internal consequences. When you get away with it, you think you're off scot-free. However, in all of these instances, your conscience, your inner voice, and the pit in the bottom of your stomach know otherwise and usually let you know that what you did was wrong.

Living with integrity is a moment-by-moment journey, not an overnight event. It takes time and challenges—real confrontations—to build a life of solid and tested integrity. It's always easy to say you've got standards, morals, lines in the sand you won't cross, but until you're in a situation where everyone is watching or the consequences are significant, you can't truly know how you'll react. You can, however, make the decision ahead of time to do the honest and correct and legal thing before you find yourself in compromising circumstances.

If you feel that you are placed in tempting situations regularly, have an internal meeting with yourself before you go. Decide your limitations. Speak them out loud to yourself. It works.

It's time to experience first-hand what this feels like. This is a simple experiment to learn about yourself and others. Check out this video for what's next:

Integrity Challenge #1

Make a list of ten times when you were tempted, and/or went against the rules. Rank each one: one point for least "serious" to ten points for "definitely trouble worthy." Don't write your name on the list. Trade with someone who also participated and rank theirs. If you can trade again (or have a small group who has participated) pass the lists around and have multiple random rankings! Post any videos/ pics and your comments on Instagram (#invisible7) and/or upload to [http://theinvisible7.com] and upon completion receive **10 points**!

Consider your list compared to two of America's most well-known athletes Lance Armstrong and Michael Phelps. Maybe your list doesn't seem so bad. Or does it?

Because he took banned, performance-enhancing drugs to boost his performance in elite competitions, Armstrong has been banned from cycling competitions for the rest of his life and was stripped of all seven of his Tour de France victories.

Phelps was outed for illegal drug use too, after a picture of him smoking pot was leaked onto social media. Both men were disappointments to their corporate sponsors. Armstrong had to forfeit a $32 million-dollar deal with the U.S. Post Office and Phelps' image was removed from the Wheaties box. Both men let down their fans, supporters, coaches, sponsors, and their individual sports. What they failed to realize is that lying is lying and cheating is cheating, no matter the size of the consequence.

Whether the punishment is big or small, your integrity always suffers when you compromise it. Believe me, I totally get human nature. I have given in to temptation far more times than I'd care to admit.

(Those stories and more will be on one of my blogs on our site when there are enough requests to know them!)

No one is above the temptations that come their way. However, if given the chance for a 'do-over,' I'm fairly certain both Lance Armstrong and Michael Phelps would go with their extraordinary physical abilities over the risk of forever damaging their integrity.

The ancient philosopher Aristotle had the insight of the ages about integrity long before cell phones and social media. He knew the struggle was real but he also knew it was doable. Consider his quote regarding a life of integrity:

"We are what we repeatedly do;

excellence, then, is not an act but a habit."

Well said, old guy...well said.

Integrity Challenge #2

The U.S. Flag is a token of the identity of our country. The military, firefighters, and police force have specific protocol for uses of our American Flag (i.e. raising and lowering on a flagpole, proper folding and storage, and traditions customary at special services). Organize a time to learn proper flag etiquette. Don't use Google! Find someone currently serving in our military or a first responder or veteran and get the scoop.

Post any videos/ pics and your comments on Instagram (#invisible7) and/or upload to [http://theinvisible7.com] and upon completion receive **20 points**!

Remember This...

"The greatness of a man is not in how much wealth he acquires, but in his integrity and his ability to affect those around him positively." – Bob Marley

"Real integrity is doing the right thing, knowing that nobody's going to know whether you did it or not." – Oprah Winfrey

"Integrity means that you are the same in public as you are in private." – Joyce Meyer

"...Survivor is about your own integrity and where you draw your own ethical and moral lines. There are no rules." – Jeff Probst

This is What Happened to Me

Prior to my speech teaching job, I was an assistant to the manager at a retail clothing store. I was his right-hand gal. I supervised the sales transactions in all departments, created agendas for staff meetings, kept track of the employee's schedules, and more. I had worked about 8 days straight and was certainly ready for my time off. I returned to work after two glorious days outside of that store. My boss walked up to me and said, "Where were you yesterday?" I said, "Off." He said, "But you were scheduled to work." Back in that day, we had cell phones, so I was always curious why I never received a call. Nevertheless, I was adamant that I wasn't written on the schedule (the schedule that I had written). He sent me upstairs to our office to go get the schedule. When I got to my desk, and looked, my heart sunk. He was indeed correct. I WAS on the schedule for the day prior. So, now what? He thought I just skipped work?

I always wrote in pencil on the schedule, which came in handy at this moment. I decided my best approach was to erase the hours I was supposed to work on the day prior, and fill it in with a "/" which was my system. Well, the "/" mark wasn't quite enough to cover up the erased hours. But, I was confident I could convince him that was the way the schedule was originally written. As I approached him in the lobby, he took one look at the schedule and chuckled as he said, "You changed it." For whatever reason, I dug my heels in and lied. I wouldn't let up. I don't know why. But, when he produced a copy of the schedule that he had made that same day (prior to my switch-a-roo) I knew I was sunk.

I got fired that day. He helped me gather my things and carry them out to my car. I ran into him a few years later at another retail store. And, I actually apologized for being dishonest. Wow. It was a huge lift off my shoulders because that incident had bothered me for YEARS!

Take it from the woman who has worked for others, as well as owning her own business... honesty is the best policy. It came back to nip me in the back side as an employer. I've most definitely been lied to about a schedule mishap a time or two. But, on either side of the coin, it just works best to shoot straight. The agony isn't worth it after fibbing – white lie or full-blown cheat!

Integrity Challenge #3

Go talk to the person in charge of Loss Prevention at your local Target or Wal-Mart. Interview them regarding the prevalence of shoplifting and the consequences for the items taken. Ask if they will share with you a specific incident. Make a list of the top five items stolen. Post any videos/pics and your comments on Instagram (#invisible7) and/or upload to [http://theinvisible7.com] and upon completion receive **15 points**!

How Will This Benefit Me?

In 2010, San Francisco Giants pitcher Jeremy Affeldt found himself in a unique situation: a simple clerical error on his contract resulted in being overpaid $500,000. That's serious money for anyone—even major league baseball pitchers! When Affeldt realized the mistake, he sought legal and personal advice from three independent sources. All three separately agreed that the mistake was in his favor and he was fully entitled to keep the additional money legally.

But for Affeldt, it was well beyond the additional money that was technically his. It was a matter of integrity. In a conversation with his agent, Affeldt reported saying, "I can't take that money. I won't sleep at night knowing I took that money because every time I open my paycheck I'll know it's not right." Affeldt's agent, Michael Moye (who also stood to lose a percentage of the money) agreed: "As your agent I've got to tell you that legally you can keep it. As a man who represents integrity, I'm saying you should give it back."[1]

Affeldt was a prime example of a man walking in integrity. When the rules were in his favor, when he could profit from someone else's mistake legally, and when no one else would have known about the oversight, he still did the right thing because he would know.

---

1 Axisa, Mike. "Jeremy Affeldt repaid the Giants $500,000 after clerical error." cbssports.com, May 15, 2013, http://www.cbssports.com/mlb/news/jeremy-affeldt-re-paid-the-giants-500000-after-clerical-error/.

Not Convinced?

"Integrity is a quality I tried to possess not only in *Survivor* but in life. It's a characteristic we can all strive to live by daily. If you practice the true principle that integrity is, it will help you get further in life no matter what your goals and dreams are. To me, it is a personal quality of fairness; it's always holding yourself accountable. We should not only try to have integrity within ourselves but with other people as well. I've had the privilege of competing at the Warriors Games™ for the past few years, and watching teens show the integrity that they have, not only while competing but also through the way they treat other people. It is truly admirable. This is constant proof that by living out this characteristic, you can go as far as you want in life."

———

Sierra Dawn Thomas
Survivor - Season 30 & 34
Roy, Utah

T.P.Q.'s

o   Do you find it easy to tell 'little white lies' if it means
    protecting your image or covering up a mistake
    you've made? What if someone else asks you to
    "cover" for their lie? Do you?

o   If you had a camera crew following you around,
    would you change how you act or how you talk? Do
    you treat high-ranking people or wealthy people
    differently than you do the janitor or the bus boy
    at a restaurant?

T.P.Q.'s

o   Is there a person in your life who influences you to do
    the right thing? Do you encourage others to do the
    right thing?

o   Do you allow circumstances to dictate how you act or
    speak or treat others?

Bonus Challenge

Write yourself a contract on how to act with honesty and integrity. Determine what is acceptable and unacceptable behavior by answering the following:

Is it ever okay to take credit for someone else's work?

_____

What about gossip? What's your personal policy on talking about others?

_____

What do you do if you find something that doesn't belong to you? (Remember the challenge?)

_____

When is it acceptable to stretch the truth? Or is it, ever?

_____

What consequences can you put into place if you break your code of ethics?

_____

Post your contract and your comments on Instagram (#invisible7) and/or upload to: [http://theinvisible7.com]

QUEST FOR SUCCESS QUESTIONS

[This is a great group activity and promotes discussion.] The goal of this workbook is to guide you to become a great leader. Character qualities are developed no matter what stage of life we are in. To build your own strengths, it is important to have a clear understanding of who you are— your likes, dislikes, wants and needs—as you go through different encounters. Answer the questions below to enhance your discovery of you!

If you could be ANYBODY famous, who would it be and why?

_____

_____

_____

Who was your all-time favorite school teacher and why?

_____

_____

_____

_____

If you could be an animal which one would you pick; if a place, where; or a thing, what would it be?

_____

_____

What is your absolute favorite activity?

_____

_____

How big is your heart (1 = smallest, 10= largest)?

_____

What filler (color, substance, thing) is inside your heart?

_____

Have you taken part in a random act of kindness recently? If so, when and what were the circumstances?

_____

_____

What was the BEST birthday you ever had? What made it special?

_____

_____

Are you on a team (sports, work, a committee, etc.)? What is your greatest strength on the team? What is your biggest weakness?

_____

_____

If you could have someone else tell your parents ONE thing that you would like them to know, that you aren't comfortable saying, what would that be?

_____

_____

_____

_____

If you could change one thing about YOU or your LIFE, what would it be and why?

_____

_____

_____

_____

_____

_____

_____

_____

_____

_____

_____

_____

_____

_____

_____

_____

_____

_____

_____

Use this space to make notes and personal thoughts about INTEGRITY.

Use this space to make notes and personal thoughts about INTEGRITY.

RESILIENCE

My *Survivor* Story...

Every day I was on the *Survivor* set was a test of my resilience.

Every. Single. Day.

Making it to the Final Three stretched my resilience like never before. I watched teammates and competitors voted off one by one. I witnessed one girl give up and quit. I saw the best of people and the worst of them—sometimes in the same day. Day after day I fought to keep my mind clear and to make smart moves and develop key alliances—all this in spite of being physically starved, mentally tormented, and emotionally pushed to the limit. Resilience was the key to moment-by-moment survival.

By Day Thirty, there were only six contestants remaining. That morning we had a Reward Challenge which meant the winners would receive a *Survivor* Spa Day, otherwise known as a meal, a shower, and a massage. At this point in the game, it sounded like heaven on earth! I was determined to win this reward.

For the challenge, we were belted to two other teammates, essentially traveling in teams of three every step of the way. We had to climb through various obstacles while carrying a bucket of water to help open a gate that led to an end puzzle. We were doing great!

As we climbed over a giant teeter totter, I was being pulled along by the strength of the two guys on my team. That is, until my foot got stuck in the netting on the surface. My body kept going, but my foot did not. I immediately felt a 'pop' in my ankle and knew something was wrong—seriously wrong. I managed to break free and keep going, but when I couldn't put any weight on my foot, I knew I was very hurt.

My teammate, Keith, heard the pop too and asked if I was okay. All I could think was that I'd made it this far—Day Thirty out of thirty-nine—and I wasn't stopping now. "Press on," I said, despite the fact that my ankle was already swelling and starting to go numb.

Unfortunately, we had to return to this same obstacle two more times in order to get enough water in our bucket to be able to open the gate which led to the final puzzle. Each time as we approached it, I would use my upper body and press off the guys' shoulders to keep the weight off my foot! The mind is an amazing tool in that you can make yourself think what you want. That being said, I was able to suck it up, refocus my thoughts regarding the pain, and focus on the prize. It worked.

When we put the last puzzle piece in place and I realized we had won, it reconfirmed that there is absolutely nothing that can stop you from accomplishing anything you set your sights on. It was an exhilarating moment—even with a throbbing, swollen ankle.

The host, Jeff Probst, asked me if I needed to see "medical." I declined. I already knew that the injury was pretty bad, and I didn't want to take the risk at that moment of being pulled from the game. The rules of *Survivor* are clear: You cannot receive any sort of medical help off-camera. Any assistance has to be recorded for possible use on the show. So, the producers were able to transport us close to the spa site, but the three of us were on our own to make it the last stretch. My daughter and Keith, the other two winners, helped me hobble in.

As we walked up the beach, the first thing I noticed was a giant glass bowl filled with shrimp cocktail waiting for us. I took all of the shrimp out and I shoved my foot and ankle into the big bowl of ice. I knew I wouldn't have access to resources like this back at camp, so I took advantage of this moment. I did my best to enjoy the food, the shower, and the massage even though my ankle continued to swell to gigantic proportions.

For the next few days, I literally crawled around camp and even had to begin asking my frenemies for help occasionally. Even showing this bit of weakness went against everything the whole *Survivor* experience is based upon. But I had to do it to survive.

At the next challenge, I was forced to ask for medical help which meant the entire world was about to witness my weakest moment in the game. To make a proper diagnosis, the doctor said I needed an x-ray but, as far as I was concerned, that was simply not an option because it would mean withdrawing from the game. Because it wasn't a life or death injury, I was allowed to make the decision to seek treatment or to stick it out. I ultimately decided to remain in the game, but the pain grew more excruciating every day.

I often think back to that turning point and wonder if it hadn't happened would I have been the sole *Survivor* and a million dollars richer? I'll never know for sure, but what I do know is that had I given up without trying to tough it out, I would have regretted it for the rest of my life. Sure, I would have much rather won the money and the title than endure the ankle injury, but I am also grateful for what I gained from the pain and the perseverance and what I learned about myself. I learned: If I have the ability to be resilient in the most extreme circumstances (like injured on a deserted island, with total strangers, starving, no contact with the outside world, and fighting to keep from being voted off!), I can surely stand up to any other battles that come my way.

Definition of Resilience
Capacity to withstand or recover quickly from difficult conditions; toughness

What Does it Mean to be Resilient?

Usually, people who are resilient are thought to be able to bounce back after setbacks and disappointments and failures. They don't let short-term challenges stand in the way of long-term goals and hopes and dreams. They see past immediate shortfalls because they have hope.

Thomas Edison, inventor of our modern-day light bulb, is a great example of resilience. He failed and failed thousands of times in his search for what we take for granted dozens of times a day: harnessing electricity. And of his many, many attempts, lots of them weren't minor, inconsequential mistakes; some were serious catastrophes. But think about it—every time we flip on a light switch, fire up the blender to make a smoothie, or click on the hair dryer, we have Thomas Edison to thank—and the thousands of failures he endured before the light bulb became a reality.

To say that Edison had a healthy and resilient perspective would be a tremendous understatement. In fact, this is what he had to say about his many attempts:

"I have not failed. I've just found 10,000 ways that won't work."

Just think where we'd all be if Mr. Edison had been too discouraged with his failed efforts and stopped after ten tries. Or one hundred. Or five thousand! What if he'd thought to himself, "This will never work. Why bother?". Or, what if he'd thrown in the towel and walked away from the progress he had made and lessons he'd learned up to that point. Or, what if he decided to take the easy route and go watch TV... oh wait...there was no TV because there was no electric service. And, there was no Internet because...there was no electric service. And, there were no cell phones because... see a trend developing here?

If Thomas Edison were not the man of resilience who persevered through trials and critics and personal disappointments, we'd all be in the dark.

Literally, in the dark.

It's time to experience first-hand what this feels like. One of the *Survivor* greats! Check out this video for what's next:

Resilience Challenge #1

Spend an entire day physically incapacitated in some way—maybe on crutches or blindfolded or with plugs in your ears. Take a picture of your handicapped self and make a list of the top three takeaways from your experience. Post any videos/ pics and your comments on Instagram (#invisible7) and/or upload to [http://theinvisible7.com] and upon completion receive **20 points**!

Everyone faces roadblocks on the way to their dreams. Everyone. No one person on the planet gets through life without experiencing some heartbreak and failures. It is how they handle these detours that separates the confident and competent and accomplished from those who don't rebound well at all. It's the 'never-give-up' attitude that separates those who experience victory and those who do not in most situations.

I'm certain you've read one or two of the Harry Potter books or seen one, two, or all of the movies. You probably know that the woman behind all those magical stories is J.K. Rowling. What most people don't know is that she could barely afford to feed her baby just a couple of years before a London publisher agreed to take on the first book. Rowling was rejected more times than she can remember, but with a small baby seated next to her in various coffee shops across Edinburg, Scotland, she persevered and continued to write.

And write.

And write.

Turns out lots of people are glad she stayed at it and didn't let the rejections of many keep her from pursuing her dream. Since the release, her books have sold more than 450 million copies and she still carries the title of one of the world's top earning authors.

Resilience Challenge #2

Visit a V.A. hospital and ask a veteran to share his/her story with you. Walk around and take it all in. You will notice sacrifice. Upload pictures identifying each man or woman you visit with including their name, branch of military service, rank, and years served. Post any videos/ pics and your comments on Instagram (#invisible7) and/or upload to [http://theinvisible7.com] and upon completion receive **15 points**!

Remember This...

o   To develop resiliency, you must be patient. You must bounce back from the toughest of situations, and move forward on your life path.

o   Avoid seeing crises as insurmountable problems. Do not allow yourself to be defeated. Simply learn from each and every experience and utilize those times for your future.

o   Your reaction to a situation is your tell-all for keeping things in perspective. Find an outlet to vent, clear your mind, and be able to keep yourself free from traumatic effects.

o   You can develop resilience in a week. Choose one person who displays a positive attitude and patient mindset and copy them. Usually it only takes seven days to form a new habit!

This is What Happened to Me

In addition to teaching in Colorado, (before I moved home with Baylor), I had been the Varsity cheerleading coach. Note to self: don't ever tell your new school administration you have coaching experience. They assigned me that job too – along with the Speech class. But, the small stipend helped my single mothering income status. There wasn't much left over every week after I paid for my daughter's day care and my new apartment expenses, but we survived on 'SpaghettiO's.'

And so, I hustled.

It wasn't long before I had established enough of a following of cheerleaders and their parents to open my own business. With my mom as a co-signer, I secured a bank loan and started what was to become the busiest cheer and dance training center in the area. I was overwhelmed at the support and reception from so many. I had to quit my school teaching job.

Fast forward a few years to when I had remarried and had another baby on the way. I knew I was going to need more help at the gym as my family grew. A young guy stopped by the gym and claimed to be one of the *best* coaches in the area. What an incredible relief, I thought! He knew how to coach cheerleading, he had a good rapport with all of my students, and he seemed super interested in the success of the gym.

Until...

until...

He talked me into relocating the gym to an area that was outside of my clientele's circle of convenience. He said all the right things about how we could merge our gyms, combine our students, and become bigger and better as business partners. I did what every smart businesswoman would do: I went to lunch with him, wrote up our partnership agreement on a napkin, and began making plans to move and merge. I pitched it to my current students, got out of my lease, and began the process of moving my complete operation to the other side of town. What was I thinking?

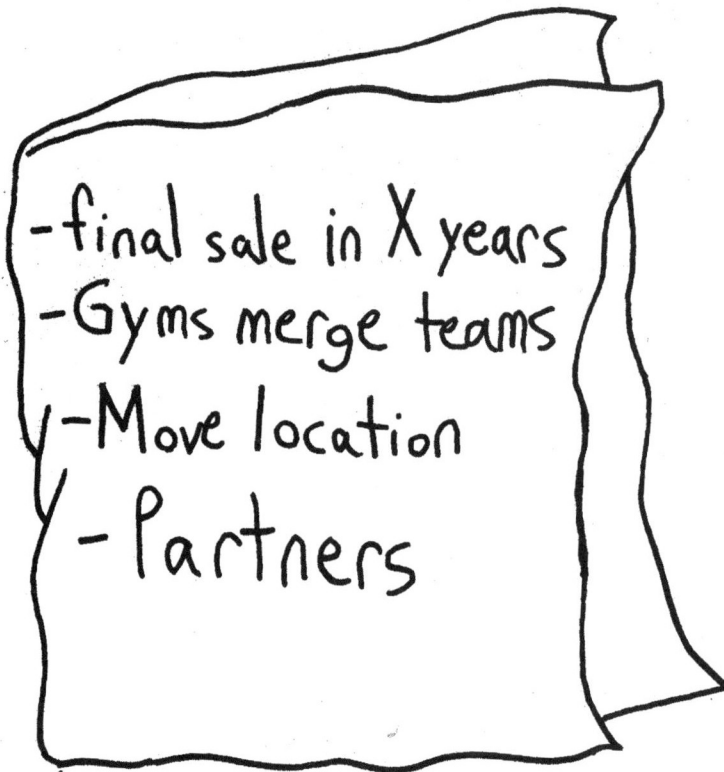

- final sale in X years
- Gyms merge teams
- Move location
- Partners

By this time, I was really pregnant, but my new partner assured me he would get the new location up and running while I had the baby and took a small maternity leave. In my absence, one of my most loyal and protective coaches kept calling me and reporting that things were not lining up anything like the agreement we made at lunch that day. There were new logos on the walls, new cheer uniforms, and most disturbing was the fact that 95% of the current students were my students, not his. He brought only 5% of the clientele to the new operation.

And then it got worse.

My first day back after having the baby I walked into the gym and I'll never, ever forget what he said to me: "You don't need to be here. You need to be home being a mom." There was one small issue to his proposal: I had no income. He had stolen my business out from underneath me and left me no way to recoup my students and their families because of all the hype he had created and sold to them. He promised his would be the most fantastic gym in town. He said his new coaching technique would take them to a whole new level in competitions. And, he said his new facility had lots more state-of-the-art equipment than our old one (which was my original creation).

I had no choice but to go to Plan B, something I always keep in my back pocket whatever the situation. I wrote all my students and parents the most eloquent letter I could. I explained that I was moving on—away from this coach and his gym. I took with me that one loyal coach - Waldo, a few pieces of gym equipment, and some office furniture. Within no time I found a place to rent twice a week and started teaching and coaching again. We outgrew the space in a couple of months and I ended up totally and completely reinventing myself, my gym, and my reputation just one block from my original gym. This new gym was so successful that, within a few years, I was offered a very attractive amount to sell it and so I did.

Resilience has served me well. I prospered financially and personally—all because I kept going and refused to allow others to drag me down.

Resilient Challenge #3

Seek out someone who has suffered from an addiction and gone through rehab and is currently sober. Ask if you can attend a therapy meeting or a group session with them as a silent observer or at a minimum – interview them. List three primary things you experienced. This one will be worth a post, because sobriety is such an amazing feat! Post any videos/ pics and your comments on Instagram (#invisible7) and/or upload to [http://theinvisible7.com] and upon completion receive **10 points**!

How Will This Benefit Me?

You can read success stories of homeless people getting real jobs, super stars who grew up poor, and severely injured people who have made miraculous comebacks. These stories are inspiring and motivating because we can all think of setbacks and challenges we've had in our own lives. When we see others who have experienced a setback, an injury, or a personal low point, but have overcome it, we're encouraged when we realize they didn't let it define them or their future. Why? Usually, inspiration shines through people who aren't quitters. It's human nature to have admiration for heroic stories. Those people who have overcome an unfortunate situation, an addiction, a set-back are really no different than we are. They simply have the self-worth necessary and desire to leave a legacy... whether they know it at the time or not.

Stephen King, Jim Carrey, Shania Twain, and the one and only Colonel Sanders are just a few examples of famous people who had a really hard situation and overcame it. And they have all enjoyed unbelievable success because they were resilient and didn't give up.

But for every Stephen King or Jim Carrey, there are lots of stories of people who quit and gave up on themselves and their dreams. Oftentimes when people don't bounce back or continue to work towards their goals, they end up feeling defeated and believing their situation is hopeless. When all hope is gone, many people turn to easy distractions that dull the pain temporarily. It may be drugs or alcohol or overeating, but the relief is the same for all of these—short-lived. When the numbness wears off, they have a choice to move forward or to return to the comfort of the short-term fixes.

Think about this: If you have an unfortunate set of circumstances that occurs in your life, how will you choose to react? Will you be resilient and keep trying or will you give up and live with the defeat? Your entire future rests on how you react.

Not Convinced?

"Resilience is a young high school girl continuing her battle to beat cancer. Or, it is also seeing one of our teens making it to the Warriors Games™ because of their hard work in completing calls to action and challenges. One of the most memorable moments was watching an incredibly strong young woman name McKay not give up, with her knuckles bleeding - fingers shredded to the bone - and tears in her eyes until she started her fire with a flint. All of them show resilience in their individual goals, passions and within each of their communities.

No matter what the challenge may be in life or on *Survivor*, there is a breaking point in all of us when one would normally opt out to failure but, instead of giving up or quitting, push far beyond this initial point of discomfort. Perhaps even when the body may quit, the mind and spirit continue to stay strong. In the game of *Survivor* there were many difficult challenges that tested my faculties of mind, body, and spirit. Discovering my most vulnerable and often most difficult times of stress taught me to rise again even knowing I will probably fall a few more times."

Joe Anglim
Survivor – Season 30 & 31
Scottsdale, AZ

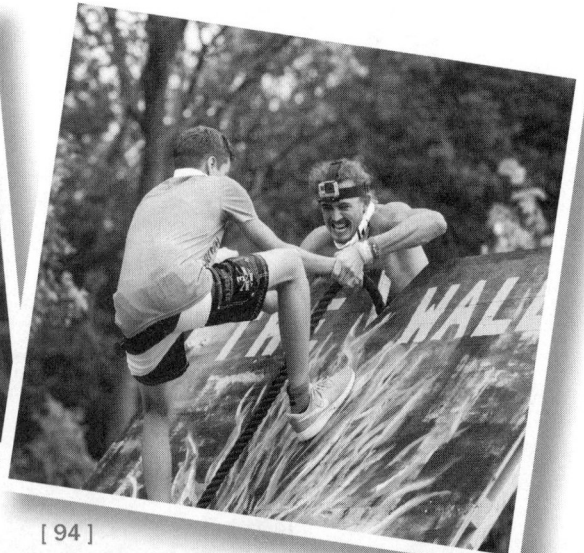

T.P.Q.'s

o   Who do you know personally who has had to
    overcome hard times? What is their overall attitude
    toward life?

o   What are the issues or circumstances in your life
    that you wish were different? Do you have the means
    and mindset to change and/or control them?

o   How do you handle the stressors in your life (i.e. job,
    family, finances, work responsibilities)?

o   Rank the hardest moments in your life 1-10
    (10=hardest)

Bonus Challenge

Choose an activity or sport that you've experienced in the past that wasn't your greatest success. Go try it again! Set yourself a short timeline and go do it once more. This would be something that you didn't get the result you anticipated the first time around and that you are most resistant to re-attempt. Create a timeline, and if possible, catalog the experience on camera. Post any videos/ pics and your comments on Instagram (#invisible7) and/or upload to [http://theinvisible7.com].

How do you navigate through the Obstacles in your life?

Activity: Drop the Rock

Goal: discovering how much weight you carry consciously or sub-consciously

Materials needed:

A large piece of paper

Pencil.

Instructions:

PRETEND you are carrying a bucket at all times (representing your life).

Place some imaginary rocks in your bucket (representing people, things that are both victories and stressors in your life).

Draw a giant bucket on a piece of paper.

Draw some rocks in your bucket. The size of each rock is according to its weight and what it represents (i.e. the bigger this "thing" is in your life... the bigger the rock and vice versa).

After you have drawn all your rocks place a weight amount on each rock.

Example:

For instance... if you are ranked the top salesperson at work, does that create pressure for you to continue to succeed? That's a rock in your bucket. You decide how big and how heavy it is.

OR, is there someone in your family who constantly requires everybody's focus due to an illness, or situation? That's a rock in your bucket. You decide how big and how heavy it is.

Once you've placed all the rocks in your bucket, you decide how long they will stay, and what size they remain. Are there ANY rocks that you could dump out of the bucket? Are there rocks you could make smaller?

With every year of your life, you grow as a person. You also come to realize what is in your control and what is not in your control. Drop some rocks; it will make the journey a whole lot lighter!

Use this page for your bucket drawing.

Use this space to make notes and personal thoughts about RESILIENCE.

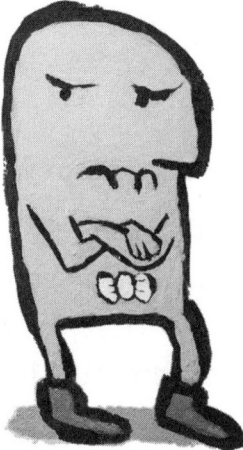

SELF-DISCIPLINE

My Survivor Story...

In order to truly come out on top of an experience like the show *Survivor*, self-discipline has to be the footing of your game-play. That doesn't mean you have to eat sparingly; that occurs naturally because your food option is one cup of white rice a day until your tribe runs out. It doesn't necessarily mean you go to bed early; you're so worn out, you go to sleep after sunset. It doesn't mean exercising daily; the challenges and the chores around camp are harder than marathon training. And, it doesn't mean stay in touch with your faith because your best and only friend is God. What it does mean is you have to stay focused and work to control your emotions, words, actions, impulses, and desires.

I remember specifically the day that one of the players, called my daughter Baylor a "brat" after he was beaten in a challenge. It floored me! I remember saying, "EXCUSE ME," super loudly! The host, Jeff Probst, tried to stir up a bit of drama and said, "Wow, Missy! Things just got real personal." I could have easily allowed that scene to escalate into an episode of "Geraldo" (which is exactly what the viewers loved!), but after a few sentences where clearly I wasn't being heard, I told Jeff, "Never mind. It's not worth it!"

Survivor pushes people into acting in ways that, in real life and under normal circumstances, they probably would not. If I took away your car, home, family, friends, phone, computer, toilet, shower, and food, how would you react? What if, after taking those luxuries away, you were put in a position that physically and mentally pushed you to limits beyond your comprehension? If you were honest with yourself, you'd probably react in ways you wouldn't necessarily be proud of.

Let me be honest—there were definitely days when I wanted to throw in the towel. Watching one girl quit on our season was bittersweet! It had a great impact on our predictable alliance—who would now be friends with whom? And like her, there were times I wanted to surrender, I think we all did. But in the end, I didn't; I relied on my self-discipline. I knew that if I wanted to cross that thirty-nine-day finish line, I had to give it my all in every single situation. I had to establish a routine in my mind in order to stay on track. And interestingly enough, that's the way life goes... or not.

Survivor was a magnified version of my life in so many ways. The people I was surrounded by represented many of the people back home—some good, others not so much. As for all the twists and turns and unexpected challenges during the game, they too were strangely like an animated version of my life path. The whole experience helped me to realize that self-discipline is truly an individual choice. It's not something anyone can do for you or to you. Just as you can't control anyone else on the planet, you are the only one who can control *you.*

During the days and nights on '*Survivor*,' I had become so accustomed to the habit of biting my tongue (when all I really wanted to do was slug someone!) that by the time I got to the final tribal council, I was armed and ready. It was a good thing, because that experience called for a full suit of emotionally protective gear. In a speech delivered by the guy who had it out for me since Day Ten, I was verbally sucker punched and sliced into small pieces. It was a personal attack on me, with my daughter sitting close by and listening firsthand to every hurtful word. On top of that, it was going to be aired on national television. It was definitely my low point in the whole experience—hearing those awful things said about me and to me while knowing millions of others would hear it too.

You know the feeling when someone starts yelling at you and there are certain words you grab onto and can't move past and from that point forward, the rest of the rant sounds like the teacher talking on "Charlie Brown?" That's what happened to me in that very moment. It took every bone in my body not to lash back out at him.

Every.

Single.

Bone.

Mercifully, it paid off. The press, my family and friends, and even a few of my cast members commented that my ability to not respond to his outburst displayed all the character traits included in the *Invisible Seven*. It was a sweet moment, even though it was only a silent victory, because I knew in my heart I had done the honorable thing. All those years of my grandmom reminding me, "if you don't have something nice to say, don't say anything at all," had finally been put to the test. And it served me well.

Definition of Self-Discipline

The ability to overcome one's feelings and overcome one's weaknesses; to pursue what one thinks is right despite temptations to abandon it

What Does it Mean to Be Self-Disciplined?

Have you ever made a point to only allow yourself to have one glass of wine with dinner instead of your normal three or four? Or, have you set your alarm to wake up an hour earlier to exercise? Or, have you controlled your mouth when someone in the office or worse – in your family- said that *one thing* about you that sends you straight over the edge?

If you've ever done anything remotely like these have to/ought-to/need-to tasks when you really didn't want to do them, CONGRATULATIONS! You've practiced self-discipline.

The whole concept of self-discipline seems so clearly obvious: You disciplining you. And while that is what it means in its simplest form, there's so much more to self-discipline and the many ways it shows up in our individual lives. The most commonly held definition of self-discipline is closely tied to willpower and self-control and inner strength and all those other words that basically mean the same thing: doing what should be done or what needs to be done in lieu of what you want to do.

Are you familiar with "Game of Thrones?" Most people don't realize it's creator George R. R. Martin worked long and hard, suffered many professional rejections, and continued to perfect his writing tirelessly before he hit the big time with 'Thrones." He worked decades as an author, steadily building up his fan base, before he received any sizeable recognition for his work. In a Forbes magazine article, "5 Inspiring Guys Who Prove Overnight Success is BS," the author explained, "He didn't wake up one day and think to himself... 'I'm going to write a script and storyline and shoot it over to HBO. I should be an overnight success in the morning.' A large percentage of the millions of people that tune in every week to watch that show probably never heard of Martin prior to the TV series becoming incredibly popular...you can't say he didn't put in the work."[2]

It's time to experience first-hand what this feels like Check out this video for what's next:

2 Long, Jonathan. "5 Inspiring Guys Who Prove Overnight Success is BS." Entrepreneur October 22, 2015: Print.

Self-Discipline Challenge #1

Choose one habit and do the exact opposite of it for seven days. It could mean talking less (or more) in staff meetings or participating when you usually don't or saying only kind words (if your usual is the opposite) or being on time everywhere or something else you could do the opposite and better yourself. Switch it up! Capture a few pictures or videos of your behind-the-scenes efforts and post with your comments on Instagram (#invisible7) and/or upload to [http://theinvisible7.com] and upon completion receive **15 points**!

The infatuation with instant gratification has become a by-product of technology. A two-hour delivery by Amazon; books, music, and movies that can be downloaded immediately; our 24/7 ability to communicate with anyone, anytime, anywhere has served to make waiting almost a virtue of the past. Still, studies suggest that when we don't buy into every opportunity for instant satisfaction, there are rewards for practicing patience and self- discipline. Think of it like this:

wait longer + work harder = more contentment

Every accomplished individual will tell you, overnight success is a myth, a lie, and a fairy tale all rolled into one. No one reaches greatness—in any arena—without committing to doing.

Everybody knows Charlie Brown, Snoopy, Lucy and Linus. They are iconic cartoon characters created by a man named Charles Schulz. He began drawing in kindergarten but his first comic strip wasn't printed in the local paper until he was 28 years old. On top of that, he had been through many art classes where teachers told him he just wasn't good enough. He had applied for a job at Walt Disney and was rejected. He continued to experience one detour and disappointment after another.

Throughout his younger years Schulz had many opportunities to take a different path, but still he pursued drawing. He looked for every opportunity to draw cartoons on virtually everything including his letters home while serving in the Army. Once he began experiencing success with the "Peanuts" characters, he didn't stop drawing and creating characters and funny dilemmas for them. He maintained his self-discipline to keep producing even when he probably would have rather been doing something else. The result, however, is that his cartoon characters are known all over the world and the "Peanuts" brand is one of the most successful of all time. Schulz proved that self-discipline can pay off big time. Extremely big time.

Self-Discipline Challenge #2

Do not text or use any social media channels for a weekend (48 hours). No texting, tweeting, Facebook messenger, Instagramming, or any other social platform. Don't respond and don't post anything. Make every communication you have with someone be verbal (in person or on the phone). Keep an ongoing record of the number of times you reached to check your phone. How much time did you save by NOT checking social media or texting?

List the top three things you experienced over the 48 hours. Post with your comments (at the END of the 48-hour period) on Instagram (#invisible7) and/or upload to [http://theinvisible7.com] and upon completion receive **20 points**!

"The only discipline that lasts is self-discipline."

– Former NFL Coach Bum Phillips

Remember This...

In order to accomplish ANY success, you have to set yourself a goal and stick to it! Here are some helpful reminders:

- o Create the SAME daily routine (every day)
- o Surround yourself with like-minded people
- o Eat right and exercise
- o Set a realistic time-line for tasks
- o Schedule in some F.U.N.
- o Mind over Matter. No matter what, you can do it!
- o If at first you don't succeed, try, try again

This is What Happened to Me

26.2 miles is a long, long way to run! At one point in my life, that sounded fun so I set out to accomplish that goal—a pretty major goal—to run a marathon. Since I felt like my life could be pretty much summed up into a daily marathon, I thought this would be a piece of cake. Boy, was I wrong!

I had my sights set on the San Diego Rock 'n Roll Marathon and I only had three months to train. Thankfully, I had already been a runner by choice for my routine exercise. When I started down this path it was still incredibly challenging. My goal was to run a marathon in under five hours. The training for this included running five days a week with a ten-mile run on the weekends, leading up to an 18-mile run the weekend prior to the race.

Between operating a cheerleading gym full time, being a single mom of two kids, and a few attempts to carve out a little bit of time for fun, training for the marathon was quite the feat. I remember when I got to the final weekend before I was to fly out to California and I still had to tackle that long run—all eighteen miles of it. On the Sunday I had planned to do it, we had one of the biggest rainstorms Dallas had seen in many moons. I did what I thought was the next best thing, I went to my local gym and climbed on the treadmill for a three-plus-hour run. My trainer friends felt sorry for me and would come by to replace my empty water bottles or throw me a new towel.

It was so incredibly boring—me, alone, on the treadmill. There were more than a few moments when I didn't think I could possibly finish. I played mind games with myself. I would "start over" every few miles and act like I was just setting out to do a six-mile run. I even ran out of music on my iPod (yep, an "Ipod"). I thought about everything under the sun to the point where I almost ran out of things to think about! But I kept going because I knew that running the race in under four hours was my goal, and that meant I had to get close to a 20-mile mark before I headed to California.

Race day was beautiful, typical Southern California weather. With the exception of having to run inside an In–N–Out Burger place to use the bathroom, I made pretty good time. That is until Mile Twenty-three.

All of a sudden, my right shin felt like someone was stabbing me. I began to limp and then I began to slow down. Around the corner happened to be one of the medic tents where I zipped in and asked, "Do you have any Tylenol or Advil? I need something to make this pain go away." I was not (and am still not) a big fan of medication, but I had my mind set on finishing the marathon in under four hours—with or without any setbacks. I took four Tylenol. The medics asked if I wanted them to wrap it, but as I limped off I yelled back, "Thanks, but I don't have time!"

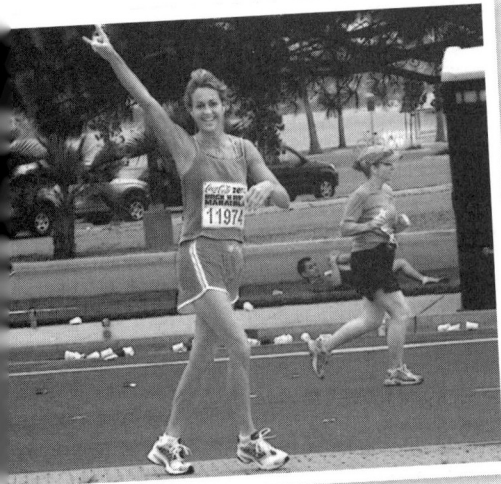

As I neared the end I remember spotting the finish line and seeing the time clock. I couldn't believe my eyes. It said 3 hours 56 minutes. I had done it! I had accomplished what I set out to do—even through the pain. Even though that was my one and only experience running a marathon, I proved to myself that when I followed my plan, I could reach my goal. It wasn't easy (and sometimes not a lot of fun). It was harder than I ever expected. However, much like making it to the final three on my season of *Survivor* (with a cast on my leg, no less), completing the marathon in under four hours showed me the tremendous power and pay-off of self-discipline.

Self-Discipline Challenge #3

Forgo all fast food (drive-through, ordering to-go, no 7-11 sodas, no Starbucks) for seven days. Tally up all you would have spent at the end of the week and donate it to a kid's charity that provides for youth in need. Post a picture when you deliver the donation with your comments on Instagram (#invisible7) and/or upload to [http://theinvisible7.com] and upon completion receive **10 points**!

How Will This Benefit Me?

Consider what can happen when a coworker starts putting in a few extra hours prepping for a big presentation. He knows it would mean a huge win for your team and bonuses for everyone involved if the client signs with your company. After a few late nights at the office, some of the other team members start to stick around and help. By the weekend, everyone on the pitch team is on board—contributing ideas, info, and manpower. When the presentation is made, the prospective client is blown away and eager to sign with your team.

And to think, it all started with one guy who put in a few extra hours to benefit the team.

This was the case for NBA Hall of Famer Michael Jordan. He was known for practicing hours beyond regular team practices and eventually his self-discipline started to rub off on his teammates. Jordan would hold his own practice at his home before he was supposed to be at the gym. Before long, most of the team was showing up early to practice, too—having a practice before practice. During his time with the Chicago Bulls, they became one of the most successful teams in NBA history.

One of Jordan's chief rivals during his pro career was Kobe Bryant of the L.A. Lakers. Bryant took training to a whole new level, frequently getting to the gym at 3:30 a.m. He even called his trainer once in the middle of the night asking if he could come over now to help him with some conditioning work. By the time the trainer arrived, Bryant had already put in an hour workout and was ready for more. He even went so far as to change his shooting style rather than sit out a few weeks when he broke and dislocated several fingers.

Self-discipline pays off in areas outside of sports too. Dallas Mavericks owner Mark Cuban hasn't always been a billionaire. As a hardworking entrepreneur with a start-up software company, Cuban regularly stayed up until 2 a.m. reading about technology and software. Besides not getting much sleep in the early years, Cuban went seven years without taking a break from the business. When he sold it at the peak of its value, he had time and money to do anything he wanted—like buy a professional basketball team.

Not Convinced?

"Self-discipline plays a huge role in the Warriors Games™ because each team is only as good as their individual player's weaknesses. What one player may think is the right thing to do for completing a particular obstacle may not be the best decision for the team. But, to be able to follow AND lead is true self-discipline. I've always heard "pride comes before the fall", and this has never rang so true than when we were going head to head to beat another team in challenges outside of our comfort zone.

On *The Amazing Race*, the strongest teams are the teams that work together and display self-discipline even when adversity hits. That's the one thing my partner, Josh, and I were able to accomplish."

———————

Tanner Kloven
The Amazing Race - Season 27
Ft. Worth, Texas

T.P.Q.'s

○ What is one goal you could set this month that would positively affect your work or home life?

○ Who do you know personally who displays extraordinary self-discipline?

○ What is one thing you might consider removing from your life that could help build your future success?

○ If a meeting was called today to honor your achievements, what would you want to hear them say?

Bonus Challenge

Create a system for virtually any goal that you set for yourself. Write down your own rules and guidelines and then stick to them. A realistic time line is also helpful to stick with it.

Some examples might be:

o   Be on time

o   Exercise regularly

o   Drink less alcohol

o   Get a job

o   Sleep better hours

NOBODY gets to change your perspective of WHO YOU ARE!

Activity: CHANGE THE TAPE!

Goal: to be able to shift negative words into positive thinking

Materials needed:

Pen or Pencil

Instructions:

Choose five words or statements that have been said to you that had a negative impact (refer to the "Icky Stickys" activity if necessary). You have the ability to rewrite anything negative to become positive.

Some people use their mouth to hurt others. Some use their mouth without the intention of hurting others but don't realize the effect of their words. When you have a clear understanding and acceptance of who you are, you will be better equipped to stay on your individual track and build your character. It is extremely important to remember that some words are derived from a person simply having a bad day and they aren't necessarily targeting you.

(EXAMPLE: If someone says:

"You are such a procrastinator. How do you ever finish anything?"

I can change it to:

"I am very careful and particular because I want to make sure to do my best work.")

Practice always brings improvement. Whether that's in how you communicate with others, how you eat, how you act and react, the more diligent you are – the better you become!

"You're a know it all."

I ask questions to become smarter

If someone says _____

I can change it to _____

If someone says _____

I can change it to _____

If someone says _____

I can change it to _____

If someone says _____

I can change it to _____

If someone says _____

I can change it to _____

If someone says _____

I can change it to _____

If someone says _____

I can change it to _____

If someone says _____

I can change it to _____

Use this space to make notes and personal thoughts about SELF-DISCIPLINE.

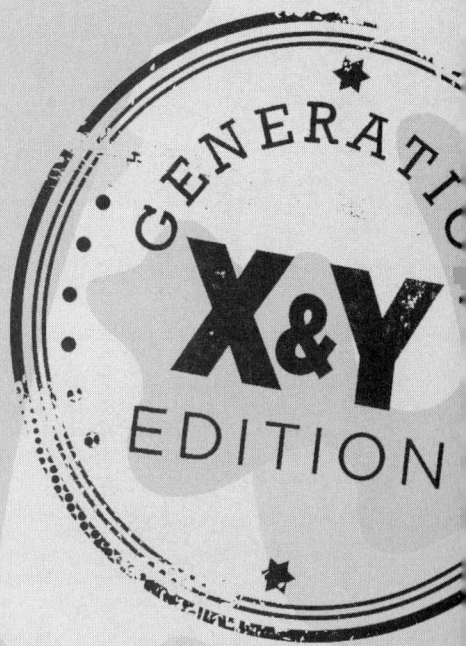

COMPASSION

My *Survivor* Story...

During my season of *Survivor*, everyone began on the show with a family member on the opposite tribe. There were brothers, sisters, husbands, wives, and close friends. In my case, it was my oldest daughter, Baylor and me. We were the only mother-daughter team, and I was really proud to represent moms and daughters as tough and capable women. One of the most unique pairs on our season was a set of identical twins, Nadiya and Natalie. On Day 3, Nadiya was voted out!

So, here's how that works: After each immunity challenge, the winning tribe is safe and returns to their camp for the evening. The losing tribe, however, is forced to attend "tribal council" where you vote to send somebody home. It was hard enough to choose that one person, but on my season there was an added amount of emotional strain being that the person going home was somebody's loved one. There was always great anticipation the morning after tribal waiting to find out whose torch was snuffed the prior evening.

On day 5, our tribe- because we had won the previous challenge- was escorted into the arena first. We watched and listened as Jeff said, "'Hunapu' (our tribe) is getting their first look at the new 'Koyopa' tribe. Nadiya was voted out at the last tribal council". Natalie started crying immediately. She explained that the bond she had with her twin was as close as a mother/daughter relationship, maybe even closer. And, she knew that the longer she remained in the game, the longer it would be until she saw her sister again. All of us could relate; anticipation of your partner being voted off created separation anxiety before it even happened.

When we returned to camp from that arena challenge, Natalie and I headed out to search for an immunity idol. I mostly went along as a shoulder for her to lean on as she worked through the shock of her sister being voted out. (My tendency is to comfort people in times of distress, even if they are playing against me for a million bucks.) When she said she wanted to find an idol, I jumped at the chance to help her.

Along the way, she convinced me to get on her shoulders so I could better reach what we thought was a suspicious looking hole in a tree. We were a bit wobbly at first, but after we got through the initial learning curve of shoulder sitting, I grabbed hold of the tree to steady myself. Just as I stuck out my arm to put inside the hole where we assumed the idol was hidden, one of the cameramen shouted, "That's a snake!" Let me tell you, that was not just a snake. It was a giant boa constrictor! Natalie swung me around and I leapt like I've never leapt before off her shoulders and away from the tree. It was crazy to believe I had almost reached in to disturb an eight-foot long snake known for squeezing people to death.

After we got over the initial scare, we both had a big laugh and it was a great diversion for Natalie. It was also an excellent lesson that helped me to realize how being compassionate can sometimes be the best medicine for somebody's sadness, plus a little distraction along the way, too.

Definition of Compassion

Sympathetic pity and concern for the sufferings or misfortune of others

What Does it Mean to Have Compassion?

Compassion and empathy are two of those touchy-feely words that often get used interchangeably and incorrectly. That's probably because most people don't know there is a distinct difference between what the two words really mean and how they should best be used. To set the record straight, here's the difference:

To have empathy means you share in a person's emotional state. On the other hand, to have compassion means you are identifying with another person's emotional mood and you want to take some sort of action to alleviate their situation...like when you hear there is a student in your child's school who can't afford to eat lunch and you work to find a way to provide.

Empathy: If a co-worker is makes a big sale and they jump for joy, you share in the excitement. If a friend goes through a breakup or gets yelled at by the committee head, you carry the pit in your stomach too. You feel much of what they are feeling at the moment but you get over it, move on, and that's usually the extent of your involvement.

Compassion: Your friend shows up on crutches and is struggling to carry her purse, you do it for her. It doesn't have to be a really grand effort. It's usually just the simple things that mean the most to people.

You can have empathy towards someone

without feeling compassion towards them;

However, you cannot feel compassion for another being

without having empathy for them as well.

It's time to experience first-hand what this feels like. Check out this video for what's next:

Compassion Challenge #1

Commit to helping someone who works in a supporting role at your office building, your child's school, your University, your health club. You can only choose a person who contributes to keeping the facility running smoothly each day, such as the cafeteria crew, janitors, security, or groundskeepers. Volunteer to help for a total of three hours within one week.

Be sure to video your experience and post with your comments on Instagram (#invisible7) and/or upload to [http://theinvisible7.com] and upon completion receive **15 points**!

On August 25th, 2017 Hurricane Harvey hit Southeast Texas, causing catastrophic flooding and historic devastation throughout the coast of Texas as well as the fourth largest city in the nation, Houston. There were over 100,000 houses damaged and destroyed. Lives were lost, entire neighborhoods were ruined, and people's worlds were disrupted for many months afterwards. However, the compassion of those able to help and least effected became known across the country. Hotels took in displaced families offering meals and shelter free of charge. Stores and restaurants that could give families a safe place to stay opened their doors around the clock. Prayer vigils were held nightly for many days afterwards as people of all faiths came together to support one another spiritually. Many of the survivors hardest hit were among those reaching out to help others with what little they had remaining. It is a given that most of us can easily relate to people in these situations, but it was the compassion of those who actually stepped in that motivated their efforts.

Compassion is necessary for the overall good of our society, our country, our world. Without compassion, many more would suffer neglect than already do; many more would go hungry than already do; and many more would ultimately die unnecessarily than already do. Compassion is the call-to-action for injustices large and small—in your corporation, committee and in Third World countries.

In January 2017, an eight-year-old boy in Ohio committed suicide just two days after he appeared to be bullied in the school bathroom. The surveillance video from the school shows kids walking right past him, stepping over him, poking and kicking him while he lay on the floor unconscious. When I watched the video, my heart poured out with compassion for the boy and especially for his mom. For some unknown reason, it seems the school didn't tell her about the incident that day when she came to pick him up. Therefore, when he began throwing up later that evening, she had no idea it could be concussion related. He later took his own life.

In the days following the boy's death, many families and students made quite a fuss after the video was released. It's all well and good that they were upset after the fact, but wouldn't it have been incredible if just one student had gone home and told their own parents about what they had seen that day. Make no mistake, there were kids who witnessed the bullying and saw the boy on the ground. One person— just one! —speaking up might have saved this boy's life. And the bullies might have been stopped before they bullied someone else.

Lots of people talk about wanting to have more compassion and many others have written about it, but here's the irony— compassion is not the talk; it's the walk. It's the I-can't-stand-to-see-the "different" guy-at-work-be-teased-one-more-day feeling that sends you over to pull up a chair beside him. If you don't act on it, just thinking about it doesn't help the person out one little bit.

Compassion Challenge #2

Participate in a handicapped sports game or activity. This could be wheelchair basketball, sleigh hockey, special Olympics baseball or any other event where you will feel as equally handicapped as the other participants.

Post a video or pic of your experience on Instagram (#invisible7) and/or upload to [http://theinvisible7.com] and upon completion receive **20 points**!

Remember This...

"Love and compassion are necessities, not luxuries. Without them, humanity cannot survive."

—Dalai Lama

"From everyone who has been given much, much will be demanded; and from the one who has been entrusted with much, much more will be asked."

—Luke 12:48 NIV

The point is not to "give" only if you're rich and famous. The point is, no matter the talents, gifts and blessings you have, use them to give back to others. Compassion for others can be packaged in different ways. Whether you have a car to donate to a single mom needing to drive to work, or you have the resources to run a winter coat drive, helping others with what you have is what defines compassion.

This is What Happened to Me

Raising my girls as a single mom sometimes felt like the clown act at the circus riding the unicycle and juggling the tall tower of breakable plates. And the old phrase, "it takes a village" is most definitely true.

So, there I was teaching and coaching as an alumni at my old school. My former English teacher was the principal. My former history teacher was the assistant principal, and the man who would unlock my classroom door for me at least 3 times a week because I was late. Mornings were rough! I would scoop baby Baylor up out of her crib and often times would fly into day care with her wearing pjs. Those incredible day care providers would take that baby from me and say "Go, go... get to work – we got her!" And, for that season of life, she had a good breakfast, incredible care-givers to brush her hair and get her dressed for the day.

She would tag along to the football games, riding in her car seat inside the 16-passenger rental van that the school provided for me to transport the cheerleaders. From about the time she could walk and speak, she, too, was on the sidelines in a tiny cheerleading uniform with poms (literally blending in with the squad.)

When I opened my first cheerleading gym, I had an overwhelming amount of students and I was pretty understaffed. Sometimes my front desk would have checks and cash piled up where parents would leave their tuition. A woman named Harriet appeared one day – and took over that front desk. Phone calls started to be returned, drawers became organized, and she brought me a homemade tuna fish sandwich with grapes every single day.

After Abby was born, Baylor had more offers for sitters, rides, meals and playdates than you can imagine. I was so busy I couldn't see straight. There were more people rocking the baby in an infant carrier, and taking care of Baylor than I knew how to thank. When I reflect on that part of my life, I am so grateful and so humbled by the incredible support of friends, family, and even strangers who stepped up to be my right hand when both of mine were tied up.

Compassion is a natural human reaction. We all want to help one another. How many times have you looked in your rearview mirror when passing that person on the side of the road with car trouble and wondered "do they have help?"

Those families and adults – and my coaching staff – saw my juggling act and stepped in to help without wanting anything in return. It was definitely a pay it forward moment for me. This season of life, I jump at the chance to assist any friend or parent with their kiddos.

Compassion Challenge #3

Write an encouraging note to someone telling them something you admire or appreciate about them. You don't have to go overboard, just a note saying what you think is cool about them. Here's the catch: the person you choose cannot be a close friend. Deliver it to their desk (if at work), or to them personally. Just to capture their reaction on film. Post your video or pic of your experience on Instagram (#invisible7) and/or upload to [http://theinvisible7.com] and upon completion receive **10 points**!

How Will This Benefit Me?

It's hard to be distressed or despondent when you're helping someone else with their issues. In fact, it's darn near impossible.

Compassion for others = contentment

This was certainly the case for Joy Bailey, a young woman from the Dallas/Ft. Worth area who had spent her childhood feeling left out and detached from her peers, often the victim of bullying. To make matters worse, Joy has been battling diabetes and all the complications from it since she was three-and-a half. But instead of focusing on all that was wrong with her life, Joy began looking for ways to help others find a sense of hope and purpose for their lives.

She began leaving anonymous notes of encouragement wherever she went—restaurants, stores, hospitals, even restrooms. She decorated the envelopes with colorful stickers, bright markers, and enticing words such as "To: You. Yes, YOU! There's encouragement inside…" Inside, the notes were filled with uplifting bits of insight such as, "I know you have a lot of stressful things going on and you may be overwhelmed, but just realize that life is beautiful. Things will get better."[3]

Can you imagine how you'd feel if you came upon a note like this right after you woke up late for work or got pulled over for speeding in a school zone? It wouldn't solve your problem immediately, but then again, it might help you keep your problems in proper perspective.

Joy eventually created a website so people could express their gratitude and share their stories of finding the notes. Hundreds of notes later, Joy has touched and inspired and encouraged countless people she has never met, yet still believes in. Since being featured on the front page of the Dallas Morning News and on local news stations, the grassroots kindness project has received tremendous support and motivated people across the country to follow her lead by leaving notes of kindness wherever they travel.

"I'm just shy and self-conscious. I don't like to have the attention because it's not about me," Joy said about her project. "This has given me a drive, a purpose. Helping a person to smile based on the cards means a lot to me."

---

3 Jaramillo, Cassandra. "How this anonymous letter writer brings joy to strangers' day." Dallas Morning News 19 January 2017.

Joy is a great example of showing compassion and she's making a difference in the lives of people she'll never even meet.

Not Convinced?

"Compassion is kindness, caring and the willingness and determination to help others in need. I like to take part in these challenges with the teens, because they possess and display all of these qualities.

It is such an inspiration to watch others giving their time and going out of their comfort zones to help - sometimes perfect strangers - get closer to reaching their goals and making their dreams a reality."

Keith Nale
Survivor – Season 29 & 31
Shreveport, LA

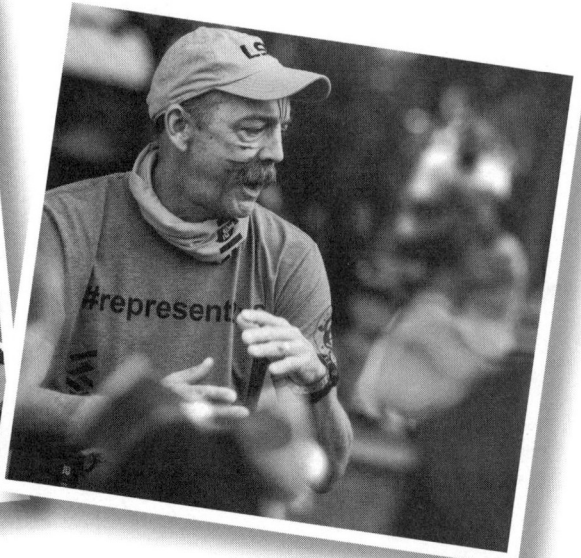

T.P.Q.'s

o   How do you react when you see someone else get pulled over for speeding?

o   What does it feel like for someone to offer you help?

o   Do you have a specific example of when you have experienced Empathy vs. Compassion?

o   Who do you know who usually speaks positively about others and does not participate in gossip?

There are people in our lives who have journeyed down the path before us. We have their experiences to be thankful for, and we can choose to take the same or different direction accordingly.

Activity: Set yourself a STANDARD

No matter our age, we can evaluate our current work and family ethics, our patterns and our choices. I like to have a map. I *need* to have a map to stay focused on making good decisions. I believe that modeling healthy patterns for others is a great way to become a dynamic leader.

Who would you consider a hero in your life? Why?

_____

_____

_____

_____

Write 3-5 things this person has done to win "hero" status in your eyes.

_____

_____

_____

_____

_____

_____

_____

What is one time you stood up for something that you believed in?

_____

_____

_____

_____

_____

_____

What is a character strength from the _Invisible 7_ which you sometimes struggle with?

_____

_____

_____

_____

What is one message about leadership that you have received from your hero?

_____

_____

_____

List something that you would like to do differently which would improve your character.

_____

_____

_____

Now, take RESPONSIBILITY and Just Do It!

Use this space to make notes and personal thoughts about COMPASSION.

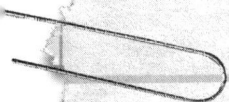

GENEROSITY

My Survivor Story...

You can't even imagine how hard it is to come back from an experience like playing the game of *Survivor* and adequately share the feelings, mental anguish, and challenges you go through on that island. One experience difficult to describe was that on the days we didn't have challenges or interviews and we would literally watch the sunrise and wait for the sunset!

We couldn't possibly discuss game strategy all the time, so sometimes we simply had real conversations about our lives. Natalie (the twin and winner of my season) grew up in the country of Sri Lanka. Before I met her, I didn't know where that was! She taught me a lot about third world countries—about the poverty their people endure as well as the enormous amount of respect and gratitude that is shown to the elderly. She helped me with the vision for a script called "Poverty vs. Privilege," which I later wrote for a youth acting camp.

As the days passed by and the further I made it to the thirty-nine-day finish line, I realized how much I would have to share with everyone back home. That's just what I did, as soon as I recovered from the lack of sleep, food, and the emotional toll it took on me. I dove straight into creating a charity to help teens afford to participate fully in their sport or talent. I poured my small amount of third-place prize money into the charity. I rolled my sleeves up and started seeking out extraordinary teens who constantly struggled to cover their financial needs for training, performances, equipment and the like in their field. This project is among the most fulfilling experiences I've ever had.

Generosity, when implemented correctly (with no expectations of receiving kudos or recognition) is incredibly rewarding. My charity, Cheer 4 Your Life 501(c)3, is currently running smoothly and can pay for approximately a dozen students a year who need funding for lessons, competition fees, uniforms and travel. The kids who are supported by our program volunteer for us at our fundraising events, show up to help at committee meetings, and always show enormous thankfulness after receiving any assistance to pursue their craft.

I believe that service to others is what generosity is all about. I believe that the giving of your time and/or money directly impacts your attitude and instills gratitude within you. Trust me on this one—I know the rewards of this firsthand.

The kids who are currently beneficiaries and those who have received support from us have shifted my perspective of my own life like never before:

The dancer, who I traveled with to Denver, Colorado for an audition (when her mom was recovering from surgery) landed herself a position in a professional ballet company;

The singer, who informed me that the first place she ever really performed in front of a large adult audience was at our fundraiser. She now sings in formal settings and in front of large crowds, with confidence on a regular basis;

The downhill ski racer, who was asked to ski with the U.S. Ski Team in Slovenia, juggles his academic responsibilities, a job, being a big brother, and carves out whatever time it takes to perfect his racing abilities;

The young soccer player who has already been signed by the University of Texas at age 14 continues to practice and play the sport as a team player, as dedicated to her club team as she ever was, never showing signs of arrogance.

There are a lot of people more qualified to do what I do. I just simply choose to do it! No matter the time it takes, and the energy to constantly ask people for funding, I would not trade my position with anyone. To witness someone else's gratitude for something to which I contributed, is the ultimate gift.

Giving brings gifts.

Definition of Generosity

To be kind, generous, and not selfish; to give liberally

What Does it Mean to Have Generosity?

You wake up on your birthday to multiple messages from friends and family wishing you the best on your big day. You receive "Happy Birthdays" on your Facebook page from friends and even some people who you don't know so well. It doesn't matter who it's from, it feels good to receive whether it's affirmations or material gifts.

Now think about a time when you sang happy birthday to someone on their voice mail, or better yet - made something original for someone you loved. Or, maybe it was a wonky-shaped bowl from your child to you for Mother's Day. Or, maybe you surprised your boyfriend or spouse by taking them to watch their favorite hockey team play on a random weeknight. No matter how you went about it isn't important; what you gave was the important thing. That's because you were giving your time, or your talents, or sending a heartfelt message. That's generosity at its best.

You've probably come to realize that, in tons of ways, it truly is more fun to give than receive. And that, in a nutshell, is the simplest, most pure, explanation of what it means to be generous.

Sir Winston Churchill, who was known to be somewhat of a stodgy, stubborn statesman, realized the value in giving generously. Apparently, beneath his gruff exterior there truly was a heart of gold when he said,

"We make a living by what we get.

We make a life by what we give."

Mr. Churchill got it right—the whole getting and giving thing, but he most certainly wasn't just speaking of material generosity. Without a doubt, all charities and well-intentioned organizations need money to operate and to make significant contributions to society, but they also need resources well beyond dollars and cents. They need manpower, they need emotional buy-in, and they need intellectual knowledge, business experience, administrative know-how, and much more. In short, generosity can be in the form of money, time or love.

It's time to experience first-hand what this feels like. Create an in-house giving tree. Check out this video for what's next:

Generosity Challenge #1

Get to the office thirty minutes before everybody else for three days in a row and hold the main door open for everyone. Or, show up early to your health club one morning. Greet everyone with a high five, a smile, and a "good to see ya." Video or snap a few pictures of some of the people you greet showing their response to your enthusiastic welcome. Post any video or pics of your experience on Instagram (#invisible7) and/or upload to [http://theinvisible7.com] and upon completion receive **15 points**!

Ben Affleck, famously known for his many roles, including Batman, poured tons of money into research for a kid named Joe with a degenerative disease after he visited the movie set where Affleck was filming. Over the course of a decade, the two became close friends. So close, in fact, that Affleck gave the commencement speech at Joe's high school graduation. Affleck's generosity didn't end there. As a special gift for Joe's twenty-fifth birthday, Affleck donated $25,000 to a children's charity that specialized in research for the disease as a way to honor Joe.

Taylor Swift is another celebrity who has become notably generous. She appreciates her fans and wants them to know it. In 2014, Swift made it a Christmas to remember when she sent boxes of presents from her travels around the world to dozens of her "Tumblr" followers. And she didn't send cheap, giveaway stuff either. Her followers received FedEx boxes containing things such as Polaroid cameras, Victoria's Secret merchandise, gift cards, sweaters, hoodies, scarves, and much more. T-Swift has made it into the stratosphere of celebrity; she just wants to be sure and thank those who have helped her get there.

Generosity Challenge #2

Gather 10 envelopes and place $1-$5 in each one. Write a note which says in your own words something along the lines of... "A gift for you – no strings attached" or "Have a happy day!" Take the envelopes with you in your car, or your briefcase or purse and had them to complete strangers which you encounter throughout the week. Post a video or pic of your creation on Instagram (#invisible7) and/or upload to [http://theinvisible7.com] and upon completion receive **10 points**!

Remember This...

- o Generosity creates chains of events that trigger upward spirals that are able to transform communities

- o Helping someone else typically makes you physically feel better

- o Giving promotes happiness, which in turn promotes real friendships

- o Generosity is contagious; start your own trend!

This is What Happened to Me

I was in the drive-through line at Starbucks and on my phone at the same time—pretty normal scenario for me. When I got to the window and was reaching to get my money out of my wallet, the woman working the window looked at me somewhat perplexed. I thought she was just being considerate and not wanting to interrupt while I was on the phone, but she had a completely different reason.

I put the phone down to pay and she said, "The woman in front of you paid for your order."

"Did I know her?" I asked.

"I don't think so," she replied.

"But I ordered a drink *and* food—that's a lot to pay for!"

And before I could gather my composure and realize the kindness of this stranger, the mystery woman was already driving away. I wanted to chase her down and thank her personally, but she was too far gone. And then I had an idea. Just like her, I could pass on the kindness and pay for the order of the people behind me! It was an amazing feeling to do something so unexpected and without any chance for recognition. I smiled every time I thought about it all day long.

You could call this a random act of kindness, which it most definitely was, but it was also an act of generosity. That one small act of kindness spurred me to get off my phone and pay attention to my surroundings a little more to share kindness with others. Since then, I have been on the lookout for anyone who might need a Starbucks drink or a snack whenever I'm out running errands. I've come to see that helping someone else is the greatest gift you can give yourself.

Generosity Challenge #3

Helping the homeless is extremely generous, especially due to the enormous amount of people, including kids and teens, who live in shelters and on the streets all over our country. Create and distribute a WEEKEND food backpack for your local homeless children's program or simply donate it to a shelter. Post a video or pic of you (and anyone who helps!) collecting and delivering your donations on Instagram (#invisible7) and/or upload to [http://theinvisible7.com] and upon completion receive **20 points**!

How Will This Benefit Me?

Being generous can benefit you like few other acts can. When we give to others, we are forced to shift the focus from us to them—and that's a huge benefit all by itself. So often, we get wrapped up in seeing all that's wrong in our lives and all that seems to be right in everyone else's. But that's not a true picture of reality. Many, many people would take your problems over theirs in a heartbeat. When you give from what you have—time, talents, or money—you quickly realize just how fortunate you are.

The more you can see the effects of your giving, the more you benefit from it. That's because it's hard to feel discouraged or dejected when you actually witness someone's gain from your help. It's a simple cause-and-effect relationship:

Helping others helps you!

Generous people are happy people. There's no getting away from the fact that a habit of being generous with others brings rewards to you. And the most wonderful aspect of generosity is that it doesn't have to be tied to your bank account. You can be off-the-charts generous without spending a penny and make a tremendous impact on the world around you.

Not Convinced?

"Generosity plays a huge role during the Warriors Games™ especially during the fire building challenge. Several people were having trouble getting their fire started. Some of the veterans came over and lent a hand to speed up the process. Sometimes it's not all about winning, it's about helping others when they need help.

When I was on *American Ninja Warrior*, I remember sitting outside the course in Oklahoma City excited but also really scared. My friend Brian came over and sat with me. It was his first time to compete also. He talked to me about sports, about the course - just anything to keep my mind off of other competitors falling. I needed someone there, and he stepped out of the role of opponent and just became human."

———

Elliott Jolivette
American Ninja Warrior - Season 8 & 9
Frisco, TX

T.P.Q.'s

o   Did you notice a difference in anyone's demeanor when you held the door open for them or greeted them with kindness?

o   When is the last time you offered to help a family member with their chores or run their errands for them?

o   Who could you bring a surprise gift to at work or at one of your weekly stops that could change the course of their week?

Service Pledge

It's time to use your own resources to show your generosity. Use this Service Pledge to make a commitment to giving back to your community, or another group which you feel needs some extra help.

If you could choose to help our world become a better place, what area of service sounds most appealing?

(rank 1-5... 5 is the MOST appealing to you)

___Feeding the homeless

___Cleaning up trash in a park

___Teaching a student to do a task or learn a skill

___Recycling products

___Singing to the elderly

___Helping handicapped people at their house

___Visiting children's hospitals and reading to other kids

___ Volunteer for your favorite charity

List something you could do to help carry out your desire.

_____

_____

Who do you need to contact to make it happen?

_____

What is your timeline goal or date of service?

_____

Who could you ask to team up with you that might have the same interest?

_____

Your Signature: _____

Use this space to make notes and personal thoughts about GENEROSITY.

**Take it One Step Further...and compete at the
Warriors Games™!**

The charity that I started upon my return from *Survivor* called Cheer 4 Your Life 501(c)3 pays for teens to enhance their training in a particular talent (i.e. dance, singing, soccer, cheerleading, ski racing, visual art). These teens also promote the character values of "The Invisible 7" by participating in challenges. We mentor and emotionally support each teen and give them opportunities to perform and compete outside of school programs to develop their unique skills and talents.

Funding is awarded for voice lessons, summer enrichment camps, audition opportunities, training, equipment and a myriad of other resources. The average range of funds distributed is $2,000-$6,000 per student per season. The applicants are not your average kids; they are focused, driven, and determined to reach a level of excellence in their arena. The students who have received C4YL funding demonstrate their ability to survive and excel solely due to this support.

For specific examples, and to hear endearing stories from our kids, please visit: [https://www.c4yl.com/c4ylkids/]

If you have completed any of the challenges in this book (posted and/or uploaded your video proof), congratulations! You are already well on your way to becoming a member of the Cheer 4 Your Life support team. I want to offer you an adventurous opportunity to help us raise *more* scholarship funds for the Cheer 4 Your Life teenagers.

There are bonus challenges available during the Spring similar to "The Invisible 7" tasks promoting more acts of service, acts of kindness and self-discipline. Ask a co-worker, professor, family member or local business owner to pledge an amount to donate on your behalf as you complete each challenge. By doing these tasks and receiving sponsorships for your efforts, you are helping a teenager continue on his/her journey to success. You will also qualify to compete at the "Warriors Games™", which is an awesome obstacle course tournament where teens and adults take on TV Celebrities. (Have you ever seen how competitive those Reality show players can be?) The Warriors Games™ is an exciting collision of *Survivor,* The Amazing Race and *American Ninja Warrior.* You won't want to miss it. Sign up at [http://theinvisible7.com] and continue what you already started today!

Oh, and each challenge that you complete in "The Invisible 7" workbook counts towards your total points necessary to qualify.

Excited to see you at the Warriors Games™ in the Summer!

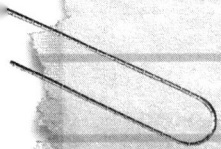